"Resilience is the catchcry of the modern world and is often harder to pin down than we think. Referring to 'how it was when I was a child', is not enough to connect with the latest generation. 'The Universe Loves a Trier' provides a practical link to the steps that young Australians can use to toughen up those risk averse exteriors that we have developed. It is a road map to recovery and discovery". **Adrian Pree School Principal St. James Anglican School**

"Ray offers the opportunity to value add to any school's educational experience in such a holistic way. He is able to cut through to students with his interesting stories and encourage them to adopt skills and values that helps them face challenging situations now and in the future". **Bronwyn Smith High School Humanities Teacher and Wanneroo Shire Councillor**

"We have been very privileged to have found Ray Armstrong as an ally and mentor for our Year 10, 11 and 12 students. His aim has been to work with us "to embed skills that students can use daily to help them maximise their potential for achievement and resilience". **Linden Davis School Principal Alkimos Baptist College**

1

"Ray's program is an excellent initiative that provides guidance to help young people navigate the challenges that life throws at them. Through his Christian approach and practical guidelines, he motivates students to aim to be the best version of themselves". **Christian Joubert Senior English Teacher**

"The teachers and students spoke highly regarding Ray and his talks and they saw some really positive growth in some of our students. We thank him for generosity and highly recommend him and his series of life values talks to any school". **Kieran Graham School Principal Quinns Baptist College**

The Universe Loves a Trier
Ray Armstrong
Copyright 2023 ISBN 978-0-646-88228-4

TABLE OF CONTENTS

Make content thy fortunes fit, tho' the rain it raineth every day." - William Shakespeare

NOTE: You will find I have used quite a few quotations in this handbook as it is impossible to convey some ideas better than the exceptional authors already have from their own experiences. Or one could say in the words of Michel de Montaigne, *"I quote others only to better express myself."* The booklet has been self-published and recently updated. However, with the best possible intent and despite my wife and I devoted literary diligence we hope it is acceptable in its current form. Please accept our sincere apologies if you discover any errors. Neither is this booklet an empirical study, it is lessons in life I have found worked for me and revealed I believe, some universal law. I sincerely hope this will give you a strong start on your journey.

My very first day of school was over and my Mum held my hand walking me home. I told Mum my teacher was Mrs Moore and then I said, "Today Mrs Moore told someone in the class they had as many brains as a frog has feathers, what does that mean Mum?" My Mum laughed and said tactfully. "It means they are not too smart, why do you ask?" I said, "it was me, Mum."

It was my very last day of school and I smiled waving goodbye to all my mates as I had done every end of school year for the past twelve years. But this time it was quite different, never had I felt so oddly alone, as there was no return for me after this summer holidays. In taking that final walk past the old brick school buildings and ovals never to return it dawned on me I was now alone in the world. No university or technical college prospects for me, no family farm to return to, no plan, no structure I was totally free yet totally scared. I was now just another young teenager in the big wide, sometimes not so wonderful world.

CHAPTER 1

THE PAST WAS JUST PRACTICE

"You can't go back and change the beginning, but you can start where you are and change the ending."
- C.S. Lewis

"YOUNG MEN AND WOMEN WANTED for hazardous journey. Low wages, bitter disappointment, long periods of being completely alone, constant danger, safe return doubtful. Honour and recognition in case of success." This is an inclusive interpretation of Sir Ernest Shackleton's advertisement for crew to join him in an expedition to be the first people to cross the South Pole in 1914. Shackleton's ship coincidentally called the *"Endurance"* was crushed by ice early in the expedition, but this failure culminated in one of the greatest endurance stories in history. The misadventure subsequently lauded as the most extraordinary story of resilience and perseverance ever recorded.

You may not be aware but you have already applied as crew for a similar journey on another vessel, the good ship, *"MYLIFE."* And guess what? Your application was successful! **So welcome aboard!**

There were a couple of people at a party and although they had just met got on well plus the added benefit of being strangers both felt comfortable in sharing confidentialities. One of the guys asked, *"How are you really?"* His new friend said. *"Well, really I am anxious about everything, feeling a bit depressed and pretty scared."* *"Well, I know how to fix that!"* the other chap said. *"The Great Gonzo is in town. Go and see him and you will laugh until you cry and all your worries and stresses will disappear."* He looked him in the eye and said, *"I am the Great Gonzo."*

Life involves risk and takes courage. Courage is defined as acting in the face of fear. And fear always lives in the thinking not in the doing. You are fearful about what might happen. However, once you choose to commit fear is defeated. You must be bold, brave even to commit and risk your own self when scared. It is to be brave enough to bring to the surface the best in you. It is the will to overcome the fight or flight response bred into us all for thousands of years.

So why do a few of us seem to suddenly thrive on the element of a challenge and others become so fearful they can literally start shaking like plugging themselves into a wall socket?

Well now we know! And you can take this first tip and start practising it, perhaps today! **Science has recently proven, anxiety and excitement are impulses released from the same receptors in our brains. We can actually choose to be reduced to a nervous, trembling shadow of ourselves in a stressful situation or we can choose to be excited, ready and eager to step up in total control. It is all up to our own choice of thinking at that moment in time!**

So how you choose to think matters.

It is your body preparing you, so the answer you choose can be YES! I like it! Now you can pause for a few seconds only, then make your choice **WILL I BE NERVOUS NOW OR WILL I CHOOSE TO BE EXCITED?** A few of these major choices in your life are called *"moments of truth"*. Don't worry, it is believed you will only have up to five of those on your journey and any adult can tell you theirs. This book is all about preparation for yours. You do not know it but you are actually walking straight into a minefield wearing thongs, shorts and a cotton Bali top! Here is a question for you? Would you prefer to be dressed in mine proof armour or carry a map to guide you right through the field to your destiny? The armour or the map?

The Map:

- ➤ Scared to make a wrong move.
- ➤ Stay the trail and be safe.
- ➤ Finish unblemished.
- ➤ You made it.

The Armour:

- ➤ Frightened but accepting.
- ➤ Pain and suffering from being thrown skywards.
- ➤ Scarred.
- ➤ Capable and adaptable.

Whichever pathway is entirely your choice.

To hopefully help you relate to what I am sharing, I have included stories of my experiences as it seems the best way for me to explain how I learned these skills over a lifetime. I believe the lessons come from what is called *universal wisdom* applicable to all of us regardless of age or time. **You see you already know these skills to be true you just do not know that you know**. The question being when will you choose to accept and use them?

Staring into the ocean not one of us Surf Life Saving Club (SLSC) members had ever seen the like. The batteries of incoming waves were like liquid mountains marching in long lines to smash the already devastated beaches of the Gold Coast. Some weary homeowners had even dumped car bodies in front of their exposed homes to try to stave off the relentless bashing from these blue monsters. A cyclone had persisted for five days delivering all sorts of junk and debris to the shoreline including the shark nets which had been anchored with old engine blocks a kilometre out in the deep. Could us thirty surf *"clubbies"* make the swim *"out the back"* beyond the breakers to have the thrill of floating over these colossal waves? Our intent being, to challenge ourselves and dive deep under and through as they cap and suck backwards, when water runs uphill. Swimming hard against the frightening drag of the behemoth was like being tied by an invisible rope and stretched taut against a log already trapped in the great roller. Only eight of us made it out, where we paused, about twenty metres past where the first giants stand up to break Most of us totally exhausted and me secretly thinking how do I possibly sneak back in? The current pushed us northwards, past Little Burleigh Hill, on which some twenty spectators now stood watching us lunatics.

Only our best surf swimmer *Macca* (aka the Penguin) had the courage to take off on one of these *brutes*. He would swim onto the crest fall through space down the face of the wave turn a somersault and spear through the wall of water deep under swim for dear life to best the undertow and the terror of being dragged backwards. Into that maelstrom of the great white-water washing machine.

Watching *Macca,* we had all strangely drifted into a tight circle! This was a subtle attempted shark safety manoeuvre rather than being on an end, believing then we all had the same chance in case *"the man in the grey suit"* (as we called any shark cruising about) showed his smile. No one amongst us was in any way confident enough to attempt Macca's skills, but of course we acted as if we could, but just chose not to. Somehow, I had unknowingly drifted in somewhat from *"the circle of love"* and in an instant found myself all alone in the *"drop zone."* Catastrophe! I found myself perfectly positioned to latch onto one of these giants. When we all heard the cry, *"SWIM!"* The horizon was moving and a huge *"set"* loomed from nowhere, the swells growing more menacing by the second as the first leviathan began to stand up. The only option being to swim with all the others straight towards it deeper out into the ocean as hard and fast as possible. The big Dutchman from the A Grade boat crew in his unmistakable accent bellowed mockingly, *"Armstrong you are kaput!"* From a distance I heard Macca yell at me, *"Don't pike!"* A piker describes one who *"chickens out"* and at our age no one wanted to be labelled a "piker". I had a few seconds to make a crucial, perhaps even life-threatening decision. Go or was my new nick name to be Chook?

What will you do when you do not know what to do? The answer to that question has determined outcomes and futures for so many throughout eternity.

Who am I? No one special, just an average trier, perhaps a bit like you and most of us out there. I am not super wealthy, nor a champion athlete. One could confidently say I was never, *"the sharpest tool in the pantry!"* So, what right do I have to give advice to you? I believe that good advice can come from those who have peered in and then stepped into or even in some cases been pushed into the abyss. They may have suffered emotionally, physically and mentally but having survived, may be well placed to give some *"battle scarred"* suggestions to others.

Believe me I have paid in full for all my life experiences and as a result I would be privileged to share with you some of the lessons life has taught me. As Oscar Wilde stated, **"Education is a wonderful thing but it is well to remember from time to time that nothing that is worth knowing can be taught."**

There is another massive wave heading your way and with this one, no one escapes. You too will be exposed and in dangerous waters but these skills can put you into a lighthouse. Strangely too, through my journey luck has frequently followed these humiliations and often turned calamity into opportunity. Now I want to show you why I believe the universe loves a trier and there is no suffering the soul does not seem to profit by.

I have had a varied career in the school of life consistently suffering from what one could call, *"a shortness of knowledge!"* Jobs like screwing lids on endless bottles on a conveyor belt in London, to being *"broke"* on the streets in Italy exhorting people to give me money for food. Working as a labourer, walking behind a bulldozer picking up sticks and leaping the odd Bungarra, making outback dirt roads in the Northern Territory. Cold canvas door knocking, been run off properties by wild dogs and wilder people. To being appointed Auctioneer of an entire outback ghost town, where bottle tops were the paving for the footpaths! On the way securing a University Diploma, lecturing at State Training Institutions and appointed State Manager for national companies. I married a beautiful, funny lady and raised two terrific children both university graduates. During this time, I have been privileged to be mentored by some outstanding individuals. In managing business teams, my sphere of responsibility consistently enjoyed national record-breaking success.

However, the best outcome for me was seeing many of my team members help me and themselves become value-based citizens and some friends for life. The question what to do when you do not know what to do has been asked of me many times. **I learned as I grew older there are certain actions which you can implement in inconvenient situations which can change outcomes slightly in your favour.** Once understood you can navigate your life a bit easier. **I often wonder what would have unfolded if I had invoked these winning values into my life from say fifteen?**

I know these *"character creators"* work and will hopefully give you a roadmap to opening many new and exciting opportunities for your future. A bit like a blueprint or template to follow. May I ask would that be of value to you? Some of my messages may resonate with you, others not so. If not, I am indifferent, I will explain why I say that later. Mind you, the life path ahead for you is like a stroll you must take through a beautiful rolling field with shady trees, babbling brooks, knee high green grass, wagtails and magpies chirping sweetly under a turquoise sky. Whilst at your feet buried a few inches under the ground lie a thousand exploding mines that could leave you shattered, battered, and sometimes splattered. But do not panic. If you choose right here is where you can secure armour and protection preparing for the time you are in the thick of life's minefield. Mind, you will step on quite a few of those *"jumping jack"* mines on the way, many strange as it may sound, as if you deliberately chose to do so! My intention is to arm you with this skillset now and in doing so be better prepared to learn and thrive in this big game called life, because that is what **IT** is!

If you choose to let life unfold you will still learn these lessons as life will keep repeating them until you eventually learn them. If you do embrace and apply these concepts now, then I feel confident you will see a wonderfully positive change. **But remember, *"if you do not use it, you lose it."* So, practicing these skills is vital.**

Let me now ask are you thinking from time to time that this whole *"gig"* of life is a bit more challenging than you realised? Please circle: **YES / NO / MAYBE / HELP!!**

No one had ever really pulled me up, sat me down and spoke the truth about real life on the outside! Does this ring any bells with you? Do you feel a little apprehensive? For example, the pressure of knowing that in a few years from now you will have been expected to decide what type of career you choose potentially for the rest of your life? More than likely in under ten years you will also choose the person you are going to partner and spend the rest of your days with! These my friends are big issues with wonderful upsides and some potentially serious downsides. So, I ask you what rating on the following question would you give yourself regarding your performance to date? **How confident would you be of your level of commitment so far?** Please be honest with yourself as the truth is a critical component. Circle the one you feel mostly applies to you?

Teachers or Managers favourite / Outstanding / Above average / Competent / Hiding in plain sight / Not Bad / Bit Overwhelmed / Battling / Can you repeat the question please?

Whichever one you circled is a fine admission to yourself and the right answer for now as we have a starting point. However you are doing up to this point is OK, because at least you are participating. As they say you have, *"skin in the game."* Your past experiences brought you to this point right here for a reason.

On leaving school, I can remember feeling like a piece of driftwood being swept along with no real direction, no discipline to get up and go to school, sitting at home as weeks rolled onwards into months. How naive was I. **If it was to be it was now up to me!** I was now in charge of my own destiny OMG! Teddy I am afraid you are going back in the cupboard behind the Grade 5 three-legged race trophy. From the day you leave school you will be entirely responsible for your own discipline and actions. No Teachers or Headmaster, so be mindful it is all up to you and **actions have consequences, as does no action.** I was a slow learner, like a blowfish never learns to leave a hook alone and always ends up flopping around on the jetty. Something else it took me a long time to understand is that the world does not owe us a wonderful time. If we sit back and expect our futures to happen for us, we soon start to see items of value being taken away from us like our energy, happiness and ambitions and we may become what is called *"mean spirited."* We may find ourselves even now falling into a category of becoming a bit of a whinger and finding a negative outlook or aspect on everything that comes our way. Others will join this party too as, ***"misery loves company."***

This way of thinking is so contagious it then becomes a habit. I know you love a challenge so try this for one day only. **Do not complain, say anything negative, whinge or bitch about anything for only one day.** You may surprise yourself! Then try two days and so on until it soon becomes a habit. Usually around twenty-one days. I slowly learned to be quiet, watch and listen for the whinging type of thought process in others then quietly disappear. I have a very good friend called Mark who I travelled the world with and no matter what circumstances befell us he would say, *"Not to worry"* this drove me to near madness which I inflicted upon myself, but things always seemed to work themselves out and these problems became matters we would end up laughing about.

Many of us too, like to play the *"blame game."* **Wayne Dyer said, *"Blame is the neat little device that you can use whenever you do not want to take*** *responsibility."* **We must choose to know we weathered the previous experiences and we elected to be stronger and more resilient for the experience and that is how we grow. One of the greatest choices we have is whether our suffering will make us a victim or a warrior. We must never be A PRISONER OF OUR PAST.** As Friedrich Nietzsche the German philosopher said, **"If you think someone has ruined your life, you are right. It is you."**

We need to muster the courage to leave behind blame in our life and playing the victim card. In my time I met many people who were resentful about what had happened previously in their life and used this as an excuse for their actions for years. They blamed their parents or their upbringing or whatever prior circumstance they could muster as a reason to say this is why I am like I am and why I act this way. There are those too who find a reason, any reason not to accept fault and in doing so use a bad experience to always justify why they acted in such a fashion. This type of thinking will bring you down, as you are still blaming the past for your current disappointments. **Your view of your past will create your today.**

In allowing these experiences to influence our actions will ensure we never really grow up. If we find historical reasons to justify our poor behaviour over and over, we are trapped in a nasty circle of play and repeat. When in fact we have learned a good lesson about who or what we DO NOT want to experience again. But be mindful THE PAST WAS JUST PRACTICE and whatever bad behaviour you continue to practice gets stronger.

There is a concept called, the *Peter Pan Syndrome* from the book by Dan Kiley based on the James Barrie classic, *Peter and Wendy*. Peter the young boy sees adult life to be a sinister, dangerous place and chooses to live with the other lost boys and girls and remain a boy all his life. Peter does not want to have to face the obligations and responsibilities of adulthood. You may feel that way too! Do not worry you are not alone. There are, *"Peter Pans"* out there today, both male, female and otherwise some in high positions of power. In my time I have seen many fail to accept the challenges and that is all they are, tests to help you grow and their refusal to accept and confront these tests stunts your own personal growth. Now unfortunately, there seems more joining the *"lost children"* all the time. You may have to ask yourself many times, *"Am I Peter Panning now?"* **If so, have a laugh at yourself and if you want, you can get over it in an instant just by smiling, acknowledge the circumstance and moving forward.** Resolving to try to accept, is what really matters and embracing the arduous as it may even become fun as you become aware in knowing thyself!

Another way to look at your past is straight from the Bible. In Matthew 11:28 Jesus said, *"Come to me, all of you who are weary and carry heavy burdens, and I will give you rest."* God bids you to come to Him and lay down the burdens you have carried in your secret place. He is there. God is calling you to be healed and blessed in humble submission to God's grace and mercy when you will find your burden removed. I can attest to this too.

G.K. Chesterton the British writer wrote: *"Anything worth doing is worth doing badly the first time."* **What he meant was just have a go at it no matter how doubtful you are or embarrassed, only try.** You may well surprise yourself and your self-esteem and confidence will grow. The more you humbly put yourself out there with a smile, the more relaxed under pressure you will become. The dividends are significant and lifelong – **so take a few more worthwhile, responsible risks,** not running with the pack is a good start. Opportunities often present themselves when you do not see them coming. And you are being asked the question by your own inner self. *"Will I stand up this time?"* The time to start stepping up is now, exactly when you know your next in the dentist's chair. **"Sometimes you may feel you are in a dark place and think you have been buried when in fact you have been planted!" - Christine Caine.** According to Bonnie Ware in her book, The Top Five Regrets of the Dying, when asked in old age what people most regret stated, *"I wish I had the courage to be true to myself not what others expected of me."* In hindsight they regret not having had a *"go"* at so many other opportunities or saying, *"No I am not in,"* knowing it was right to stand alone.

I was managing a group of eighteen franchise offices and twenty-eight company salespeople when I heard on the grapevine there was a massive property some 150 plus hectares coming on the market vacant land which had recently been rezoned to residential.

Meaning all this land was now suitable for housing and now worth a fortune. Whilst it was not in my job description, in a way I justified that it was still real estate. Of course, to win the opportunity to sell the land we would be competing against the biggest and best commercial brokers in the country. I made an appointment for ten minutes with the Director in charge of the enterprise for this public company. I guess he was curious and he asked me, *"Why should we be the ones to offer you the property for sale?"* I looked him right in the eye and slowly said, *"I want to impress you."* He seemed to immediately understand my commitment. We won the Listing. I was elated. The National Manager of our firm in Sydney became aware in twenty-four hours. He could probably hear me whooping from Perth! He told me to be on the next flight to Sydney and in his office at 10am the following morning. I bounced out of the elevator at 0955 with a grin like an African meerkat at sun up.

"Who the hell do you think you are? You are only a mule!" boomed our national leader. I was struck dumb, in an instant, *"from a rooster to a feather duster"*. He knew the enormous responsibility we had now undertaken.

The Sellers had already called him asking him to draft and oversee a detailed weekly report from me, which his secretary was frantically assembling involving streams of paper and sticky notes. Producing in the end a mammoth Excel spreadsheet. We went to a national Public Tender and four months later I sold the land for $105 million. The largest sale ever by our firm. Never doubt your own ability even if others may. **Courage is what you do, not what you say you will do.** Failure only shows us the way by demonstrating what is not the way. So let us get planted not buried and start challenging ourselves!

Those mistakes already made and those nasty experiences you may have endured were only pre-season trials for you to learn lessons. I know there will always be those who seek to use their past as an excuse, who hide behind their history to avoid taking responsibility for their actions. But I will not be one of them. I am a person of character, a person of integrity, a person who keeps their word and takes control of their life. Knowing who you are now, what you stand for and how well you think you are going right now,

however good or bad is important as your change begins NOW.

"He keeps pressing my buttons so I eventually react." That means you have a button to press! Together we will remove that button.

This self-awareness is something to become expert at. It is said the two most powerful words in the language are *"know thyself."* This little book is all about the one person in the entire world you could speak most fluently about if you were asked – **YOU.** Remember that statement, who is the one person in the world you could speak most fluently about? Of course it is **YOU.**

Summary:

- I can choose my reaction from now on in pressure situations. I can choose to be nervous or I can say "NO, I CHOOSE TO BE EXCITED!"

- I will stop myself immediately if I am found whinging, complaining or criticizing others.

- How would I honestly rate my level of effort / commitment so far in life? Would I give myself a 50%, 60%, 70%, 80%, 90% or 100%? It may be interesting to revisit this question in six months.

- I am not A PRISONER OF MY PAST as now I accept the past was just practice and I have started a new beginning.

- I willingly step up to challenges and take on positive actions I never usually would. *"An Oops is better than a what if"* - Varun Mitra

- I am prepared to promise myself to take on the armour of difficult life skills outlined in this book and to push myself further than ever

28

before. Remember, *"You can be scared of failure, but you should be terrified of regret"* - Deshauna Barber.

Please choose one action and start practicing.

WIFM: You have finished the first chapter. I hope you are curious enough to continue our journey. I was going to explain the following at the end of this book but thought the beginning or near enough may be a better choice. **WIFM** – is an acronym for What's In It For Me! **What is the payoff?** Well, this is my promise and guarantee to you. If you allow these skills to become part of your character you will:

➤ **Become a higher achiever in life and your chosen career**
➤ **This is difficult to explain but there will be a meaningful change within you with growing influence and goodwill**
➤ **Be regarded as a person of compassion and respected**
➤ **You will be on a pathway of awareness with the infinite**
➤ **You will become luckier**
➤ **Use it or lose it. If you do not practice the skills, they will leave you**

CHAPTER 2

SILENCE IS GOLDEN

"People will forget what you said, people will forget what you did, but people will never forget how you made them feel." Maya Angelou

My Mum used to say to me, *"The wise old owl he sat in the oak, the more he heard the less he spoke, the less he spoke the more he heard – why aren't we all like that wise old bird?"* The philosopher Rousseau put it another way, *"the person who knows a little talks a lot. The person who knows a lot keeps quiet. The person who knows a little considers everything they know to be important and wants to tell everyone. But the one who knows a lot also knows it is possible to know a great deal more and will only talk when other people would like them to."*

May I ask would you like people to like and even respect you a little more? Let me ask you why are some people driven to buy the fanciest cars and clothes? Why do so many of us want a home larger than we will ever need or driven to make more money than we will ever spend? Or randomly spray graffiti, post criminal acts boasting on social media, get excessively *"inked up"* with tattoos, join an outlaw motorcycle group or do outrageous things and look back and think OMG!

Because everyone wants to feel of some value and some go to extremes to appear so! IN FACT, THE MOST PRESSING DESIRE OF NEARLY EVERY PERSON ON THIS PLANET IS – TO FEEL IMPORTANT OR VALUED. Kings, Presidents, champion athletes, millionaires and garbologists all want one question answered in a positive fashion, *"Did I do OK?"* That is, *"Am I of some usefulness in the minds of others?* **And the opposite of that the worst feeling is to be ignored. Or as I have suffered from time-to-time RDS (relevance deprivation syndrome!). You simply do not matter.**

How do we make someone feel important? A good start is whenever you talk to someone try to say something good about them, it is not hard and people will appreciate being appreciated! *"To get recognition give recognition."* This is a golden phrase. **Give them a genuine compliment. Not false flattery nonsense, think of what they are good at or how they look and**

tell them. Every time you meet someone say something simple and encouraging about them like, *"You are always smiling or always good to see you?"* This simple action of giving recognition has a profound effect in developing relationships. **People will always remember how you made them feel.** Conversely what would be the most hurtful thing you could do to another? Ignore them.

Now please allow me to add to the above by giving you the third piece of vital information in my initial recommendations If, when meeting other people in conversation ask questions about them and have them talking about themselves, the most remarkable thing will happen. **They will love you for it!** *"Talk to a person about themselves and they will listen for hours"* – said the greatest self-improvement coach ever Dale Carnegie.

At school I used to frequently stare out the windows so much so I had written on my School Reports, *"his daydreaming is an ongoing issue."* Let us try a little exercise. As you are reading this book you may be thinking this guy is full of it! Or I'm starving, or when is he going to get to the point? Or he may have something I can use here? **So how or what you are thinking right now is how you have managed and run your life up to now.** *"The way you do anything is the way you do everything,"* – Martha Beck. If only I had focussed totally on what was being said in class my future could have had so many options open to me. Be mindful start practicing this skill of total attention and watch how often you wander off!

What I am now going to ask you is surprisingly difficult but life changing! **Let them finish!** STOP INTERRUPTING! It is said the ability to listen with pure intent is the most precious gift you can give! **From now on when you are with anyone, in particular your teachers, focus and genuinely listen to them. In class, at home with parents, in every moment focus 100% on listening to what is being said and not butting in with your say. This is not easy.**

Plus, in conversations try to always call people by their name. This is a terrific way of establishing relationships – but it is challenging, as you will want to stop them, interrupt and have your say, sometimes without the courtesy of first using their name. Be aware. I have found **that all the smart people are great**

listeners. The finest negotiators in all fields purposely engage the other person and have them doing the talking. I guarantee you will make good friends and learn so much, as the listener not the talker will always win the day or as Will Rogers, the wonderful American commentator and comedian said, *"I never miss a good chance to just shut up."*

Also, when you do talk, pause first, do not speak fast, talk slowly, then you really will have your listeners attention. Remember we were given one mouth and two ears.

I was attending a discussion my daughter was having with a car service mechanic about some unsatisfactory work on her vehicle. My daughter asked to see the Manager who was aware of the problem and ready for her. Then she let him speak without interruption for four or five minutes, until he just ran out of reasons and excuses. Then excruciating silence, not a word, until in resignation he said, *"OK I am happy to refund you the monies in full."* I said that was well negotiated and she responded, *"Dad, you know the one who is silent has the power."*

To demonstrate, try this every time someone speaks to you and watch what happens:

1. Always turn your feet to face them so you are forced to look at the person.

2. Lean slightly forward.

3. Turn your head down slightly towards your shoulder and listen. (This body language has proven to demonstrate empathetic engagement).

4. Look the person right in the eyes.

5. Listen with intent, I mean really listen.

6. If they stop, ask a question about what they said or wait and say nothing.

7. Stop thinking about what you want to say.

8. *"How beautiful it is to stay silent when someone expects you to be enraged".* - Paul Coelho

Over the years as I learned to **listen more intently,** I was slowly recruited into the subtle, *"reading people business,"* as the less I said the more interesting things they revealed to me.

Ever notice how some people seem to whine a lot? I mean they are well and truly set up in the fault-finding business. They complain, argue, reject, block and criticize all out of habit. **Do you want to take a massive** step forward in your life right now and be happier? Become NON-JUDGEMENTAL It is that simple but so hard. You never judge others and give voice to a negative opinion about someone else, you accept and let it pass. It is important to understand when you judge another it is your ego trying to assert control. Ego is pride the Bible's greatest sin and that can gravitate into hubris. Then you are in real trouble! At this stage your ego has taken control, thriving on the status and conflict on board a runaway train, hissing and screeching down to anger and depression. Your ego can kill all your aspirations! Be humble and act with grace.

"When I am tempted to criticize I will bite my tongue; when I am moved to praise, I will shout from the roofs". - Og Mandino. Humility is the key.

However I believe there is one proviso here, rarely you will bear witness to something patently wrong. Remembering the old adage *"for evil to triumph it only takes a good person to do nothing."* Then you must act.

As mentioned in the previous chapter did you challenge yourself not to complain or whinge! Start making it a habit. See if you cannot be negative or

judgemental about anything, not complain or deride anyone or anything. You may be surprised how often you respond with a negative, pessimistic attitude or cast judgement. Force yourself to stop, be silent and bite your tongue! You may have noticed how difficult this is even by lunch time!

What are you really made of? The next few crucial years of your life are when you have the time and freedom to take some leaps of faith. Over this term you will have the relative freedom to choose among the vast array of options open to you. Later, life becomes more complicated and available choices can be constrained. The realities of work, family, resources etc, can limit choices. Employment is not as secure as when I was young, with the new global village driving for ever-increasing efficiencies in this digital world, redundancies and contract labour being widespread. Indeed, seeking new careers five or more times may be standard operating procedure. Even potentially working from home full time. A job sure is harder these days.

So do not be afraid of having a try at anything that you know is an honourable challenge. I remember rowing surf boats in carnivals and other crews trying to row us down on the way back to the beach. We would be totally spent rowing on sheer willpower. In a boat crew one cannot just stop or slacken off. The entire unit requires perfection in unison and when asked for 100% whether you like it and can do it or not you must step up for it. At these times when we were threatened our crew captain (the boat Sweep who stands in the stern) would say quietly, *"Crew you are being asked the question."* Coming home exhausted and rowing because the crew kept rowing, I used to think, *"Hey, what a time to ask me a question!"* The question he was really asking was, *"Now let us see what you are made of?"*

If you do not dig deep and seize the moment, that moment of growth of your spirit is gone forever. Here is your chance, from now on, when you feel there is nothing left, just hang on and give anything you do your best try. So what if you do not initially succeed or even mess up. At least you stepped up and had a *"crack"* and gave it everything in that moment. Win or lose that is when you change, and the growth happens.

One of the most astute decisions you could ever make to set yourself up for success in life and build your character is to join a rowing club or any activity-based team club will be good for you. For example, in rowing the sum of the parts is greater than the whole. You become an indispensable component of a machine that demands perfection in silence, strips all your ego and delivers the absolute best in you. *"Rowing is a funny thing. It's not just a sport. It's an outlet for pain through pain. It's a teacher of discipline and determination. It takes you to your breaking point and teaches you to bend rather than snap. It marries grace and power. It makes you strong. It gives you friends. It's your psychologist and second home. On occasion it's been known to save someone from themselves. Yes. Rowing is a funny thing."* (Author unknown).

My younger brother won a Head of the River in the first Eight. He was a man at seventeen when I at eighteen and a half was still a boy. And terrified if in six months my number would be called up and I was inducted into the Army and probably off to Vietnam. I once saw on a T shirt, *"JOIN THE ARMY - travel to far away, exotic places, meet strange, different people – and kill them!"*

For example, one of those land mines I mentioned previously could be your social media footprint or that tattoo which says, *"Stops at all Stations."* Many employers in their diligence engage *"Matrix"* like applicant tracking software programmes, diving and searching into your posts on Facebook, Instagram, Tik Tok, X and the like. Whilst your job application is simultaneously screened by another algorithm for sentence structure, grammar, specific relativity to the actual advertisement and a subtle psychology test thrown in! Your preparation in this area must be second to none or the system will say, *"computer says no."* In fact, many never realise, when they win the role, they are simultaneously being tested in the probation period and watched from on high by those who make the major decisions. **As you are every day, right now**. A bit like a brand-new player thrust into a team where everyone wants to see their level of commitment to the group, their objectives, and their ability to get the job done. So please be mindful the question they are seeking to answer is what do you have under that veneer you portray to the world? Particularly how well you handle pressure situations. Even when you are silent there is a lot being unsaid about you. **Everything you say or do or how you look and even stand (like hands in pockets)**

is making a statement for those in the reading people business. So firstly, I learned we may be even better off first reading our own selves.

When I was young, I was like the rabbit in the spotlight dashing madly every which way to try to avoid being shot in the cotton tail! Hopefully, you can learn early now from a lifetime's experience zigzagging to help you choose ideas and actions that may enable you to become a confident, balanced and successful person. Someone who is valued for those most special aspects – honourable, being there for someone when it counted, trustworthy and courageous.

Could you become someone who in the process of living, gives away some small value to all whom they meet every day? A sort of Paladin. Please note I make no distinction here between male and female. A Paladin by the way was a holy knight and the bravest, most respected in the court of a King or Queen. Paladins were blessed by God and were in other words people with that most beautiful and elusive possession, so few ever find – **Grace.** How to define grace? A few clues may be revealed in later chapters. But I am afraid you will have to source your answer to that on your own.

Apprentice Paladins let us just take this journey of self-discovery one step at a time. All I ask is you commit to accepting knowing you will be uncomfortable and challenged. You may also consider fast tracking your learning with added fun by forming a small group of like-minded souls, as aspirations are easier to achieve when there are two of you with similar goals. There was a large sign at the Australian Sports Institute in Canberra. *"When you are not preparing well someone else is – and when you meet them, they will win."* That applies to your schoolwork, your sports, and your future. This book is a form of preparation or training now for life **– Out There**. Being out there is extremely competitive and can be ruthless particularly for the *"newbies."* You see many teenagers honestly believe that when they are released from school all will fall into place. Confidence and enthusiasm are great achievements, but so are overcoming life's tests and trials.

Just prior to printing this booklet I bumped into a young man who two years earlier attended and that is about all, a few of my discussions. He was a confident, sassy *"rooster"* which certainly made an impression.

After the class he came up to me and we had a chat, he advised his career was certain and all mapped out focussing on the world of developing computer game technology. When I saw him again, he was on trial in a restaurant, for a job picking up and washing used plates. The bravado and self-assured nature were gone. I was quite shocked. I enquired how things had worked out so far? He responded in the most telling short sentence, *"I wasn't ready!"* Funny how much he reminded me of someone I knew better than anyone at that age! **Now the young man is learning the lessons and building resilience.** The entire objective of this manuscript is to start preparing you for the game ahead. How ready you will be is totally your call. If you can takeaway only one or two new habits or life skills that will be enough, **because sooner or later we all pay a price and learn the rest.**

May I ask what you will do when you are confronted with challenges like:

- Alcohol, drugs that are offered by *"friends"*.
- A physical relationship
- Bullying
- Being left out
- Anxiety

- Disappointment
- Anger

If you are easily offended you are also easily manipulated. So, you need armour and armour you will have. Please be mindful once you walk out of those school gates you will have no more structure, no more timetables to keep and only **the discipline you choose to instil in yourself.**

I can recall after leaving school getting up at 9am, then 10am and eventually 11! A hearty breakfast, casually look for a few job roles, watch some TV and before I knew it time for a nap! My circadian rhythm or body clock was striking thirteen! This is a guaranteed way to skew your thinking and invite lethargy, bitterness and blame into your life. So, you need to be *"kitted up"* including a routine and a plan. Otherwise, like I was you will be sitting around these days on your phone and or playing computer games, becoming more quarantined from reality and quietly discouragement will come knocking. Incidentally six months later how did I snap out of my cosy little cocoon? I joined a surf club and didn't that rip off a few band-aids! You may also wish to invoke **The Rule of Seven** a communication concept devised by Dr. Jeffrey Lant. The principle being with these tips, I would like you to repeat the action mentioned (e.g., becoming a great listener) seven times in the next couple of days so then it will be embedded into your mind and or pin a copy on your wall. **But it is difficult, however knowing it is not going to be easy makes it somewhat easier if that makes sense?** It is important you understand that point, you see if you know something is going to be a challenge your mind will help ready you for the event and thereby make it easier to do. In the book *On Becoming a Person* by Rogers and Kramer the authors talk about **"The Paradox of Change - *If you can accept that a task is difficult somehow it no longer becomes as difficult. Then the curious paradox is that you will change."***

I have another subtle objective to achieve in our journey. I want you to become a quiet leader. Do not worry, **just follow the steps and it will happen.** Leaders are listeners, they stand strong and stand up for their values and the values of others. Leaders calmly embrace all these skills and inspire others by the way they view and live life. **We need to instil and build in those key values, so now the past is behind us as it was just** practice, the new you starts from now, as before you know it, you too will be Out There.

Summary:

- I am going to become the best listener I know and ask questions to engage people. I will focus on attentive listening particularly in class.

- I will act on the Rule of Seven and write down, speak or action these new skills seven times to make sure they are instilled in my life.

- I talk slowly with intent. I am non-judgemental. It is my ego trying to gain control.

- "How beautiful it is to stay silent when someone expects you to be enraged". - Paul Coelho

- Join a club or any activity-based organisation outside school, find new friends, new purpose, inner strength and the best of myself.

- I am willing to become a leader. I prepare to be the best I can even for the next six months. Never forgetting leaders always go first.

- Leaders are listeners, they stand strong and stand up for the right things.

- I let people finish talking - I do not interrupt!

- I never criticize, when I am tempted, I bite my tongue and respect and happiness will follow. Unless that one circumstance arises when your values demand you act.

- I keep my ego or pride under my control. Locked down. I act with humility in all I do.

- *"People will forget what you said, people will forget what you did, but people will never forget how you made them feel." -* Maya Angelou

ACTION PLAN

1. What can I do to become a better communicator?

....

....

2. I will practice daily and have some fun by not criticizing others and being ruthlessly non-judgemental?

....

....

4. What are some clubs I can approach outside school?

....

....

Which one will I choose to launch now?

CHAPTER 3

OUT THERE

"The only thing that ever sat it's way to success was a hen." - Sarah Brown

Will you be ready when the time comes? I was so far behind the pace I could have been still sitting on the school bus! But fortune smiled upon me. Two years after leaving school two of my Rugby mates had booked to go to London and see the world. I was at a bit of a loose end - that is code for job and prospects none. I did however have some savings, so I thought I would love to be in this *"gig"* as well. I persuaded them to allow me to tag along. At that time my one best friend jumped in as well, not an easy decision for him too. He was only engaged to be married! Probably best we were leaving the country as my fault for telling him I was on the trip of a lifetime. Four weeks later the four of us little *"munchkins"* were sailing out of Sydney Heads. Off like wide eyed, white mice into the great unknown, north of the Tropic of Capricorn. To give one an idea of how naive we were, in Fiji the four musketeers decided to dine out at a fancy restaurant. I had pledged to have a traditional meal at every port so ordered the Turtle Soup. It was a magnificent table setting and as I gracefully pushed my soup spoon away from me sipping the delicacy I remember thinking. *"Gee this soup is rather bland."* A few minutes later the waiter showed up at my shoulder grinning from ear to ear. I was about to tell *"the garcon"* I had *"elegant sufficiency"* when he placed another bowl next to mine. I had been elegantly spooning the water in the finger bowl!

Swanning through the pool area of then one of the world's most prestigious hotels, *"The Acapulco Princess"* things were on the up and up! We lasted about eight minutes before being escorted back to the entry by a couple of huge moustached Mexican *hombres*. Our brand-new XXX size rainbow Sombreros and a wild stab at a room number must have cruelled our pitch.

On arriving in London, I secured what I would call a speciality appointment as for this role left handers were in demand. I was screwing lids on jars and passing to the right all day long a product called Oxoid (a form of beef extract like Vegemite). The working hours in the UK were quite different. Arrive at work, clock on at 8:30 then to 9:15am a full hot breakfast. Then twisting my life away for an hour. 10:15 to 11am a forty-five-minute morning tea, saunter back and hard at it now dunking and slipping thick, wet, red plastic bands on the bottle tops. 12 noon to 2pm lunch when the hooter would sound to wake us all up or the boys would cease ping pong. Oddly many would then feel the sudden need to head off to the lavatories with a magazine. Then vat watching as the huge cement like mixers churned the black goo to a molasses like paste. 3pm to 3.30pm a quiet afternoon tea. Looking busy *fiddlefaddlying* for an hour. At 4:30pm to the locker room to change, 5pm clock off and *"exhausted"* head home on the London Tube.

Suffering tea toxicity and ennui from the *Dickensian* conditions I decided to upgrade my standing and became a Lifeguard at Lambeth pool. At around 4pm daily a cohort of the smiling, sweetest 10-year-old boys and girls would come skipping through the doors. Full of life, laughter and an unnerving confidence. Little did I know each one had the training of a seasoned guerilla fighter. Swanning around poolside looking masterful in my whites, with these kids I spent most of my time nearly blowing the pea out of my Acme Thunderer whistle. There was also a mystery to be resolved. Every afternoon before closure I would end up on all fours carefully removing broken glass from the used toilets, totally blocked after soft drink bottles and whole rolls of TP had somehow fallen in and topped with you know what! I decided to recruit my little band of brothers and sisters and asked them to keep their eyes open for any indiscretions they may witness particularly involving the toilet receptacles. Their surveillance produced one suspect, old Dot the cashier who they could not bamboozle with their slick change tricks at entry. Lifeguard / Lavatory cleaner, learning to be versatile.

"When a man is tired of London, he is tired of life."- Samuel Johnson. Never a truer word spoken. The longer we stayed the more exciting layers this city revealed to us. But of course, as our monies diminished, I was eventually compelled to move. I departed this wonderful town as continental Europe was only twenty pounds away! I was off and on a second-hand Triumph

Trophy 650 motor bike sold to me by a Cockney *"geezer"* on the QT (quiet)! In fact, he looked remarkably like Fagin from Oliver Twist speaking in a soft whisper during the whole transaction, making me feel like I was being offered a special once only deal. I already had a reputation for being ripped off in every port, but somehow, I knew this classic machine for only 200 pounds was my ticket to adventure and home! With only the indomitable spirit of youth to back my naivety I headed off with my rucksack and a Jerry can full of fuel on little racks tied to each side on the back of the bike. Motor bike licence? Who needs one of those where I was headed! It was my plan to travel overland with a new English friend and his little 250 Suzuki all the way to Darwin and home.

Just over the Channel in Paris at the famous Pont Neuf (new bridge built 1607!) we were having coffee admiring the passing parade, when surprise, surprise my mates ex-girlfriend suddenly appeared from London and back to the UK they went. So just like that, I was on my own, abandoned and left peering up at one of the world's most magnificent cathedral's called Notre

Dame. Which surprisingly now looked like a huge huntsman spider. More on this little venture later.

Prior to embarking on my overseas jaunt, I met a bloke who was to become a friend for life. We were both training for Rugby in a swimming pool! He was an A Grade Rugby League player, studying to become a priest, worked part time on radio and it turned out an Australian surf lifesaving champion to boot! Greg Lawson persuaded me to join his Surf Lifesaving Club on the Gold Coast. I was so impressed by him I decided it was time to try for the deep end of the pool.

The surf club members came in all shapes and sizes of all ages from cheeky kids who had never worn shoes before high school, to fully grown hard-core Police Officers and Vietnam war veterans. There were boys who came from wealthy families with big coastal holiday homes, others who hitch-hiked from areas eighty kilometres inland. Thus, a real mix of personalities and attitudes and me with a toothbrush and shampoo I became aware I had come from quite a privileged environment. On weekends we would all live together at the club house on the beach and sleep in the same bunkroom. With hindsight it was a bit like visiting, *"The Addams Family"* or I would imagine joining a rascal Foreign Legion with no quarter given or taken, but always in fun. However, of all these terrific and colourful, knockabouts at the top of the tree were the tough-as-teak A - Grade Boat Crew. There was a joke, every new club member first had to stand against the club house wall and withstand bricks being thrown at them, those who did not duck went straight into the boat crew!

These, *"Boaties"* were a separate reality, men of men, a few with hair where no hair had gone before. Not like a faction or an aloof cohort, more like a quiet, tight pride of lions who seemed to enjoy an unwritten law that the rest of the club members (including our Australian champions) were there just to make up the numbers. On command any sixteen of us minions were at the ready to carry the four-man surf boat back and forward from the beach at the boaties' behest. In fact, that boat was better polished and maintained than the Chief Instructor's antique Bentley. One of the blokes in the A crew was a big, loose-limbed, muscled up fellow called Frank Douglas. He was tough as nails and carried a peculiar quiet confidence. To top it off, he and the Club captain who was also the Boat captain had recently returned from serving in the Vietnam War and the rumours where they were certainly not in the rear counting blankets!

You could say Frank was a man's man and he loved playing this game of life. Frank would always happily pitch in no matter what the task, even doling out the baked beans at breakfast with our jokingly ex-Michelin chef *"Bugs"* who was actually an ex-army cook. Everyone found Frank's method of serving a real laughing matter, feigning being *delighted* in having orange baked bean slop cascading onto us and the odd beans even onto our plates! Whatever the size of our portion that made it onto our dishes we were eternally grateful. I felt intimidated just looking him in the eye as his, *"in your face"* gaze and his easy laugh were a bit scary. On the beach I used to just keep my distance playing *"chasey"* in my event the Beach Flags.

One Saturday we were having a club BBQ at Frank's home and some wayward real *"Bikies"* decided to join us! Frank explained to them at length he had not received their written RSVP's. However, after seeing our *"lamingtons and lemonade"* one Bikie decided to jump the front wall of his residence and suddenly, Frank's party was being, *"gate crashed!"* We young blokes and the few others lucky enough to have girl friends had no idea what to do as these were heavy, rough men. All of us immediately frozen with fear, knowing a violent outcome was more than likely. Subtly and silently, Frank was moving and in one swift sweep he had grabbed this *"Bikie"* by his leathers right off the top of the front wall. Then literally hurled him forward headfirst through a hard wood trellis blooming with thorny bougainvillea. Down and out! One of my mates said to me, *"Did you see that? Is Frank some sort of Commando?"* The other two Bikies were last seen beards flowing with one leg in the air! Frank then retrieved the hapless bikie from the bougainvillea and deposited him unceremoniously on the footpath. It was a bit like watching a favourite movie, a totally disciplined demolition by the easy going, always laughing, Frank the Boatie. No real damage done and a lesson learned by both Bikies and us.

In that moment I saw a friend who alone had made every effort to make the peace, then when given no option standing up for us all. Taking on huge responsibility at what could have been a terrible personal risk, defying the odds and in fact handling a potential nasty situation with what one could almost say seamless discretion. There and then time had slowed and I saw the person I wanted to be. The only question, was I prepared to pay the price?

The values displayed by Frank the rower in that moment are universal and apart from the physical prowess apply in the same way to all of us. **Stay composed, be aware, stand up for yourself with respect, maintain your own standards and do the right thing.** The reason I relate this story is it is a particularly promising idea to find someone you respect and admire for all the right reasons, like a wise owl. Generally, it is someone older. Ask them if from time to time you may give them a call or catch up seeking some advice. **A bit like another Paladin or a Mentor**. If you have no one to go to explain how you are feeling, that can be tough. You may not even find the solution, but when you share a problem it always seems to help. My first mentor was my *"Uncle Jack"* Handasyde.

I was a partner in a business which was foundering as we were all quite adept at sales but could not manage a *chook raffle*. As a result, we had many partner / managerial issues. I sought Jack's advice. He responded in one colourful sentence. *"Ray you can only hold a poisoned pup for so long before it dies in your arms."* When I finally worked it out the clarity that statement gave me! I gave away all my shares to the other partners and this later proved to be one of my better decisions. Nearly all high achievers have a person in the background to go to when faced with big decisions or just to talk to about *"stuff."* I learned so much, his and others advice was invaluable and indeed changed the course of my life quite a few times.

Think of someone other than your parents and even ask Mum and Dad for their opinion of a friend of theirs or seek out a school Teacher, Grandparent, Uncle or Aunt to maintain contact with now and later in life. You will never regret this I assure you. **When you find your Mentor look at the qualities you like in them, and**

you may want to try to apply some of those attributes to yourself? I can remember being quite successful back in my twenties, doing well in business with a real spring in my step, as we are in our prime. On a rare occasion one day I was sitting across from my father in our lounge room wearing a denim shirt, Levi flares and the coolest pair of Italian leather sandals $40.00 could buy. I had been happily sharing some of my successes for some ten minutes. Dad listened silently, looking intently, and smiling at me then responded in a most peculiar way, which I have never forgotten. *"Son you are a mug!"*

I was shocked as we had never had any real grown-up conversations before. I stopped, perhaps right here was a lode of wisdom to be mined from my own Dad and yours too for that matter. How right my Dad was everything was going my way, but strangely enough events can and do change quickly! Even for the *super smart* like me, nearly going from *the penthouse to the outhouse* in the next twelve months as the economy crashed!

I often wonder and regret why I never sought his or my Mum's counsel over the years as I discovered both had been through times that were unimaginable to me. For example, a World War which Dad never spoke about – ever. And when I was on Christmas school holidays we would rent a beach house for a few weeks. When at the beach I remember the rare occasion Dad would take his shirt off. Revealing these long, jagged scars on his back and front like the mark a stick makes when drawn over the almost dry sand and one leg was like black marble from the knee down. Mum told me Dad had received the *"last rites"* (which means you are certified as about to die) at three separate times, one of those being the day I was born in one hospital, and he simultaneously was passing away in the Greenslopes Repatriation Hospital. I have his two Christian names but reversed as he was never expected to even hold me. Yet he came back to us. In hindsight it seemed we were always in a taxi going up to the Veterans Army Hospital. Mum told me some stories he endured which made my head spin, including operations with no anaesthetic. Whilst my Mum's father also suffered being machine gunned through both legs at Gallipoli, he too survived.

I could have learned so much from both parents had I just asked for some quiet time to explore a few matters as they came up. As Mark Twain said, *"When I was a boy of fourteen, my father was so ignorant I could hardly stand to have the old man around. But when I got to be twenty-one, I was astonished at how much he had learned in seven years."*

You may wish to open up and share some thoughts with Mum and Dad or a parent approved Mentor sooner rather than later. In fact, I have an exercise for you! **Ask Mum and or Dad to sit down and tell you, their story. Ask for some examples of when they had been challenged in life? What were they like at your age? Were they popular? How studious were they? Did they feel their life had some purpose or meaning?** I am sure you and they will be surprised.

There is truth in the maxim, *"as you think so it shall become."* Never underestimate the power of your own thoughts for as surely as night follows day what you think about will eventually manifest itself as you have willed it to happen. So be aware of how you think. **One of the best ways to prepare yourself for the world is to accept responsibility.** Sadly, I know people who were never prepared to accept the weight responsibility placed upon them, firstly by exams, then jobs out there. Being unable to control their impulses in spending and pay their own way. As a result, they became unhappy souls, as their life had no meaning. They were Peter Pans, some for life. Today sadly there are many, particularly little boys in grown up bodies some making big decisions on all our lives.

I was pretending to be someone of significance at a surf carnival and joined a group intently listening to a man called Keith. When whoa, mid-sentence, he started twitching and shuddering whilst loudly letting fly with a strange language like a Kalahari bushman, *"Nic nic nakema!"* Then Keith kept on talking as if nothing had happened. He suffered from a malady called Tourette's Syndrome. This lifelong affliction would crush the confidence of many souls. Keith *"Spazza"* Hurst was one of the greatest surf lifesavers in Australian history, mostly in a role which involved virtual nonstop shouting of instructions as the Captain / Sweep of champion boat crews! Despite Tourette's he also became a State Manager for a multinational company, was admired and respected by all who knew him. Some of the finest people I have ever met had every reason to be bitter and miserable due to the hand the cards of life had dealt them, of no fault of their own. But made another choice.

However, many of these men and women curiously seemed so much more accepting and to have become happier in this life through accepting and living these experiences. Whereas they could have easily chosen to be bitter and even toxic individuals. The world is a scary place for all of us, but as you are hopefully learning **when we practice anything, in time we start to become competent and when we become competent, we become confident and - we grow and keep growing!** For example, there is a concept called The Rule of 100. If you spend 100 hours at any particular task you will emerge as one of the very best in that field. Your skill level will grow exponentially the more you practice. The key is to do small things consistently. Very few can. **Give this a try! Take on one specific task for eighteen minutes only a day and practice the same action for thirty days.** Say practicing a kick or some aspect of study or instrument. By the end of the thirty days, you will be an absolute top performer. Every world champion I have read about practiced longer and harder than his competitors. For example, as a boy the greatest boxer Muhammed Ali used to be first at the gym and last to leave seven days a week. He would also box more rounds in the seven days prior to a title fight than any other boxer who ever lived! Thomas Edison who invented the light bulb said, "I have not failed 10,000 times I have found 10,000 ways that will not work." Helen Keller lost her sight and hearing at nineteen months old. Imagine a world of total darkness and complete silence? Helen wrote fourteen books becoming one of the top **most influential people** of the 20th Century. She had a coin struck in her honour around her face was inscribed, *"Words the spirit of courage."* They had set goals and never wavered.

Alternatively, the problem with searching for monsters is they follow you home! Will you take that alcoholic rocket fuel, or*"wonder"* drug or commit that act? All of which could very well lead to dire consequences. Will you have the discipline and courage to say, *"thanks but no thanks"* and stand by that decision, if necessary, on your own? Will you also be there down the track for those who said, *"Yes"* when they are all alone?

No no no no no no no! Outside school in particular. **I want what is called "A HARD NO" to be your response out there through these next few years in which many destructive requests and temptations will come along.** "No, I don't do that!" "No, I don't go there". I want you to say NO more than you ever say yes. In fact, most of the time just the hard NO will do the trick. Studies have proven when you say a strong NO there is a physical change in your body. The self-hardens, it instils determination in your mind creating immediate grit.

Oddly YES has the opposite effect. **The disciplined version of yourself is the best version.** You are making a stand, your character is being shaped and it will be of much more benefit not to participate than to be influenced and buy into actions you already know may have severe downsides. So, deciding what not to do is just as important as deciding what to embrace. Addiction has been a major issue in our societies for ages. It comes in many forms from Krispy Kreme's to Crystal Meth. Billions are spent on ways to help sufferers bring balance back into their lives. How is it so many know the potential lifelong outcomes yet persist on inflicting this life taker on themselves and not say one simple word? **NO! The moment one says NO a change happens in you. The dice has been cast it cannot be rolled again.** Your mind becomes laser focussed. It is like picking up and placing on you the armour of a Paladin. Your self-esteem and character shines and others see strength. In the next ten years know when you should say NO. This will become one of the finest skills to learn and make you one who stands apart with values. Please take my word on this matter. The power of your own will is remarkable as it takes root and grows. **Every day of your life will you have an opportunity to ask yourself this question; *"Today will I be a victim, a fool, or a lion?"*** Below is a slightly varied but revealing exercise for you to consider devised by business performance consultant Edmunds Paterson Director Richard Paterson. I discovered the diagram left on a whiteboard at Ballymore the Queensland Rugby Headquarters. It is fascinating over the years in business how accurately it has matched existing personalities prior to change. And identified potential "jets". **Please state which category most suits you now.**

OK HIGH SELF ESTEEM

SURVIVOR	VOLUNTEER
PRISONER	QUESTIONER

Low Care Factor (left)   High Care Factor (right)

BRUISED LOW SELF ESTEEM

Volunteer- A person with high self-esteem and a high care factor for others, who is willing to take on challenges.

Questioner – A person who does care about outcomes, but their ego is a bit bruised, they have been hurt in some fashion. So, they ask for tasks to be justified and must be convinced to take on challenges.

Survivor – A person who is confident with a good self-belief but not really concerned about outcomes, does just enough, happy to sit under the radar and go with the flow.

Prisoner - A person who is not confident, low self-esteem and avoids participation.

By the way at eighteen I would have fitted nicely into the Survivor category. Healthy self-belief but never given 100% to anything in my life. My aim is, if you are not already, to become a Volunteer.

A good thought to ponder is, *"If you have to eat a frog it is best to do it first thing in the morning. If you have to eat two frogs eat the biggest one first."* Mark Twain

However, first you need to accept one undeniable fact: **Life will challenge you over and over and those face offs will be the making of you.**

Summary:

- Who do I genuinely admire for their values? Who could I use to emulate their approach to life and ask to be a Paladin / Mentor?
- As I grow, I will keep an eye out for a Mentor.
- I acknowledge I am going to be challenged so I will be prepared and accepting when circumstances go wrong.
- A HARD NO will be my answer whenever my values are questioned.
- The disciplined version of myself is the best version.
- I will do the same task for eighteen minutes every day for only thirty days and see the results push me to another level.
- I am a Volunteer with a high care factor I support others when I can.
- Every day I will ask myself, *"Today will I be a victim, a fool, or a Lion?"*

ACTION PLAN:

What are my takeaways from this chapter which may better prepare myself now for transitioning into a more productive life?

1...
....

2...
....

3...
....

4...
....

Which one could deliver the best outcome if I started practicing now?

CHAPTER 4

LIVING IS BEING CHALLENGED

"It is by going down into the **abyss** *that we recover the treasures of life. Where you stumble, there lies your treasure."* -- **Joseph Campbell.**

On departing from London to discover Europe, I quickly discovered that it was much more expensive than olde England. My *How-To* book was based on $20.00 a day budget, mine was less than half. To help supplement my existence, in Milan I teamed up with a fast moving and even faster talking Mexican American who informed me he was doing all right, *"making action!"* Having learned how to talk when something special is on offer by copying my old cockney mate the motor bike salesman, I quietly queried from behind my hand. *"So how does one make the action?"* He slipped me a copy of a crumpled note written in Italian which translated to English said, *"I am a homeless, marooned English sailor who needs "mangiare" to survive. Could you please spare me 1000 lira?"* Shoving me into the back door of a crammed bus for a free ride to the Piazza del Duomo in the city centre I had a curious feeling, back in the US Gomez may have been wanted by the law and nobody else! He told me to, *"hit the bricks"* and look forlorn, which was not hard. My new *"amigo"* said to hand out this piece of paper to everyone in the central business district of Milan. One of the worlds fashion capitals. He recommended I do a bit of a *"jig"* for effect as well, but I just stuck with looking forlorn. In an instant reduced to begging but laughing all the way and unaware of the resilience manifesting itself.

The student was so excited about seeing the young butterflies emerge from the chrysalis that she pleaded with the teacher to let her take home one of the cocoons to watch the metamorphosis. Finally, he relented and gave her a jar with the cocoon inside with the instructions, *"Please just let nature take its course."* After a day, the chrysalis started to crack as the caterpillar inside was transforming into a beautiful butterfly, then stopped. A day later no change. The student watched and waited but nothing was happening, so she decided to help the process and broke the hard shell open a little. The next day she returned to school with the jar and the dead butterfly. The teacher asked what happened? Then the teacher explained, *"When the cocoon is breaking open it takes time for the wings to fill with blood, so the butterfly is strong enough to break free and fly."* In helping this process, the young girl inadvertently killed the butterfly as it opened too easily.

Here is something to contemplate. Psychotherapist M. Scott Peck in his wonderful book, *The Road Less Travelled* said, *"Life is difficult. This is a great truth, one of the greatest truths. It is a great truth because once we truly see this truth, we transcend it. Once we truly know that life is difficult—once we truly understand and accept it—then life is no longer difficult. Because once it is accepted, the fact that life is difficult no longer matters."* So, if we can admit to ourselves our own challenges / difficulties we are already on the way to overcoming them

Life is beautiful, but make no mistake, life will take everything you have and push you to your absolute limits because that is how it works. Life will cut you open and expose what is inside. So, we want to build you internal scaffolding of steel. Every one of us is taken to the edge of the abyss. Only when we jump and fall and get up again do we grow. At times you will feel you have nothing left in your head apart from the breeze of a gentle northeaster – but that may not necessarily be a bad thing either. Until you just crash through or fall again and again and again and get up again and again until you get **"IT"** grow with the pitfalls and hopefully have a good laugh at yourself.

The voice boomed across the company Board Room, *"Crocker my good man you are now in intensive care, in fact right now you are being measured up by our funeral directors!"* Every Monday at 7.55am she grinned at us from the wall and our fear and trepidation grew exponentially as we *"hot footed"* it down the corridor. Past the island girl in the original Matisse painting smiling so playfully. Our sales staff meetings were always held in the luxurious award laden Board Room. At the head, smiling the way a Caesar may have, mulling over a forlorn gladiator's fate, sat our leader. In his field he was the owner of the most successful, privately owned business in Australia. The team were all first-class operators, but we all knew our employment was based on the POPO dictum – *"Perform or piss off!"* On this day he had two in his sights Crocker and staring directly at another colleague Sally. Then he added. *"Switch on right now miss, because you are in the Departure Lounge and your aircraft is leaving in fourteen days to free up your future."* Some would break down in tears, others would be shocked into silence, occasionally one would stand up and head straight for the door knowing it was over. A few would take a very deep breath. **In hindsight I loved working at that firm because the discipline and clarity the boss imposed upon us created a team determined to excel at levels, we never realised we could achieve.**

Now we are going to take on some scary, apologies exciting challenges, where you will stumble, get back up, persist and even, given the opportunity, really reach out and learn to metaphorically play the saxophone or my wish the bongos! Henry Ford said, *'If you think you can or you can't your right."* As it is always the thinking of the doing not the doing that stops us. Time to start stepping up.

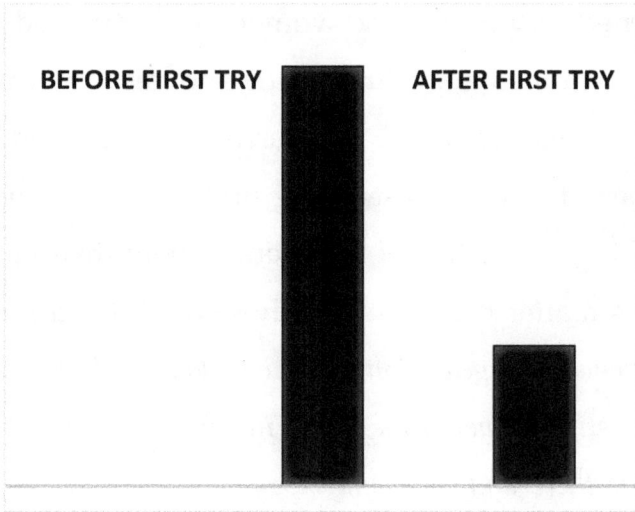

| BEFORE FIRST TRY | AFTER FIRST TRY |

DEGREE OF DIFFICULTY

Imagine knowing once you are turned out from school and reach nineteen your date of birth will go into a barrel with some balls and if you are *"lucky"* your number will be drawn and you have no say, you are off to fight a war. In a foreign country against an *"enemy"* who has been at war for generations against countries just like yours, who always just wanted theirs!

This is exactly what happened to some of my good friends, off they went to Vietnam. Returning home, not to musical bands and celebrations as in previous wars, but in many cases to torrents of abuse from many of their own age group. And these young, returned servicemen and women, some maimed for life had to immediately find work and resume a normal jovial existence, as if the horrors of war had never happened. That was stepping up to real challenges. In speaking with a few of my friends about their handling of this matter they all basically said, *"What we saw and experienced ranged from total boredom to being literally scared stiff, momentarily frozen in time. But we had to deal with it there and then and move, sometimes very quickly. Coming home we had to do the same with our lives and accept and again move on as life does, irrespective of how we felt. Despite some people reviled those of us, who had managed to live through it."*

You do not have to talk to someone for very long to start listening to a story of misfortune. In every family there is always some form of problem being managed. It may be a sick relative with cancer, a failed relationship, financial matters, drugs or alcohol. No one is exempt we all must live with suffering.

"Life is suffering"- This is the first Noble Truth of the Buddha written some 2500 years ago. Think about those words, they are as powerful now as when written

by this great teacher. **Now think for a moment and accept that your life is going to be challenging and you are going to know real, debilitating pain.**

Pain is also a great motivator. So, be aware is it the way you are thinking causing you the pain? Are there too many negative what ifs? You may frequently need to address how you think as you may be giving yourself an uppercut to start every day! *"Life is 10% what happens to you and 90% how you react to it."* – Charles R. Swindoll. **Now you know one thing for certain you can expect frequent setbacks along your journey. So, when it happens, you can say to yourself, "I was told this before so I should not be surprised, I never saw that coming, but it did - now I accept, ADAPT and deal with it."**

The funny thing is that once you acknowledge the problem the seed is sown to accept and overcome the negative effects. Also never think you are being singled out because as Socrates stated, *"If all of our misfortunes were laid in one common heap whence everyone must take an equal portion most people would be content to take their own and depart."* So, trust me we all receive our fair share. You are not being dispensed an additional allotment, life wants to, *"ask you the question!"* The question being how strong is your will? Life is trying all the time to make you stronger.

I recall the great motivator Tony Robbins listening to a young lady who was lamenting how cruel life was to her, with no job, no partner and totally disillusioned with the world. Tony asked what her childhood was like, and she sparked into life saying, *"Mum and Dad gave me the best upbringing ever, I never wanted for anything."* He simply responded with one word – bastards! In fact, sadly this young lady may have been set up to fail.

In one of my earlier forays in business many were called but few were chosen, as times were tough. Resilience became a necessity and was often expressed by the following expression, *"Some will, some won't, so what – next!"* when despite our best efforts some deals would be lost. Which means no matter how hard you try sometimes you will simply lose, if that is the case, so be it, just keep going.

A bit like asking a girl for her number. I recall once feeling so rejected I decided to see how many girls I could ask to join me on the dance floor before being accepted. I got to thirty-six. Strangely I was so accustomed to being knocked back I just went for it and the thirty-seventh who said yes was not only beautiful but we got on terrifically. Two lessons learned, persist and nothing wrong with aiming high. I also learned my favourite opening line probably needed a bit of work. *"Hi, my name's Ray how am I going so far?"* Have you given it your best shot and lost? If possible, find out why, remedy that, then – next! You must become a little philosophical and accept the result, learn the lesson, and just let it go and move on.

This is hard. Do not become bitter and resentful, dwell and ferment upon it. Just take it on the chin, which is what people like you do from now on - one must get used to being indifferent or accepting about life's *"exploding mines."* So now you are going into any day knowing it could be difficult, that makes you more prepared and therefore more resilient, aware you may be kicked in the backside today and tomorrow.

What is more many times that kicking will not even be your fault! If you can just have a laugh, as you are being sent a high importance mental email and it may very well turn out to be the best thing that happened to you. **Those that are quarantined or protected from adversity, challenges, and kicks up the rear end, simply fail to grow up.**

In case you were wondering the Four Noble Truths of Gautama Buddha are:

1. Life is suffering – (so accept many occasions will not go your way and accept that with good humour)

2. All difficulties are caused by the ego / desire – (run hard as you can for the tape and still be satisfied with the outcome. Selfless rather than selfish)

3. The way to happiness is to remove desire – (*"Only by surrendering to humility can you gain wisdom"*: - Buddha)

4. The above is achieved by following the eight-fold path – right thought, right speech, right actions, right emotions, right effort, right livelihood, right concentration, and right meditation.

This is some of the most succinct and profound teachings ever and followed as a way of life by some 400 million people. Life is challenging for all of us, there are no exceptions.

On a Monday morning, a mother went in to wake up her son:

"Wake up son. It's time to go to school!"
"But Mum, I don't want to go."
"Give me two reasons why."
"Well, the kids hate me, and the teachers hate me too!"
"That's no reason. Come now get ready."
"Give me two reasons why I should go?"
"Well for one you are 52 years old. And for another, you're the Headmaster!"

Now this anecdote may seem fanciful, but I have met quite a few of us who are like the above, carrying a condition called, *"emotional immaturity"*. Which means when matters get tough, we simply cannot control our emotions, we become all indignant, play the victim card, sulk for a while, become angry and resentful, do you know what I mean? I certainly do! The reason being, emotional immaturity yearns for carefree days of childhood, as we always want to go back to when our lives were simpler. Some people even stay and act this way much of their life. In fact, into old age. As they have never faced the realisation the world was not made to suit their every whim and the real world can be an unforgiving place for those who fail to accept, live with the setbacks and keep going.

In the great book *The Prophet* by Kahlil Gibran - a woman asks about Pain, and he said:

"Your pain is the breaking of the shell that encloses your understanding.

Even as the stone of the fruit must break, that its heart must stand in the sun, so must you know pain?

It is the bitter potion by which the physician within you heals your sick self.

Therefore, trust the physician, and drink his remedy in silence and tranquillity:

For his hand though heavy and hard, is guided by the hand of the Unseen,

And the cup he brings forth, though it burns your lips, has been fashioned of the clay which the Potter has moistened with His own sacred tears."

I urge you to read this book. When I was a bashful nineteen, a good mate who was becoming a catholic priest told me. "*If you want to really impress a girl, give her a copy or better still quote a couple of lines from The*

Prophet by Kahlil Gibran." (Knowing I would need a few I acquired twenty-three copies and still have twenty-two!) We know the pain is coming, how we choose to accept it is totally ours to determine.

Protecting people from events and problems does not make better people it makes them more insecure people. They grow up to find when things go against them, they simply cannot deal with it and revert to their childish insolence. The author Joseph Conrad said. *"Facing it that's the way to get through it - always facing it,"* not by shirking growing up, trying to cloak by withdrawing or venting your feelings with emotional outbursts or running away and or hiding in alcohol or drugs. This is how some people fail to *"grow"* and in fact abusing drugs and or alcohol are two of the best ways to make sure you never really become a true grown-up. Indeed, if you see yourself or a friend going down that road, reset, recalibrate, and grab that handbrake! As it goes from a taxi ride, to being strapped in, then on board a jet taking off - with no pilot. Kindly watch others and watch yourself.

Now imagine if everything that ever happened to you and caused you pain turned out to be the best thing that ever happened because of what you learned and how you grew as a person? To begin, along with practicing becoming an expert listener, it is equally important to begin your quest to redefine yourself.

The lesson being, as by experiencing and transitioning through the pain of the event with some form of drug, you never mentally grow and allow your real character to develop and flourish. And you will not get very far without character. Character is essential for individuals to grow and character beats talent every time. The major reason people turn to abusing alcohol / drugs is they cannot manage their perceived troubles, they simply cannot cope so they escape the pain through what they call *"self-medicating"* - and it works! But there is a hook and that is when one sobers up the pain returns as you have not accepted the reality and in acceptance grown through the pain. And it is not easy!

In fact, by denial of something which gives you momentary comfort or quarantines your real feelings, strength in the growth of your character happens

exponentially. Whereas giving in short circuits this growth and sometimes creates a habit you never want or need. A close friend Daren is a lead singer in a band for thirty plus years. He has witnessed the adventures and misadventures of an entire generation and once said to me about drugs, *"You think it will be OK. You think you can just try it. What you do not understand is that it rewires your brain. Drugs compress all current and future happiness into those moments, so that is all you will want and when not high you feel worthless or unsatisfied living in a life without meaning and many go back to that happy haven."* Drugs make us imposters.

We must be able to hold the line, our line. The truly resilient say with a smile, *"Pain is weakness leaving my body."* I used to repeat those words to myself when suffering during exercise like long runs. Also, *"this is good for me"* have a bit of a stagger, then try to have a bit of a laugh. As otherwise my thoughts and the temptation could have ground me into giving up. It is tough facing the real world but trust me the benefits on offer for those who just face it are real. I have said that phrase, *"face it - just face it"* hundreds of times to myself over the years and it works. Yes, it costs momentarily and, in that pain, I am convinced you grow. The benefits as you become a stronger person make the pain just a memory. Our football team Captain used to say prior to starting training, *"Tonight boys the pain we generate will be sheer bliss!"* **If you can have a laugh at your situation no matter how much pain you are in, you will start to take control of your life and good fortune will surprisingly start to come your way. So, you could say you will just become luckier.**

I was at the surf club and we were all getting dressed up in our finest for a night out. The guys were up to some mischief this time wedging a full bucket of water above the partially opened door of the Chief Instructor who was also a more than capable boxer. I said, *"boys I am out, as I do not want to turn back into the same mug I was before my world trip."* They all cracked up and made me never forget that statement for years!

I also believe one of the main reasons many do not seem to grow up is their deliberate failure to accept an adverse outcome, take on board the reprimand, learn the lesson and **forgive.** As Mahatma Gandhi said, *"The weak can never forgive, forgiveness is the attribute of the* *strong."* Your resentment serves no purpose. I know people who have held grudges for a lifetime always only causing bitterness because it is your old arch enemy - pride coming to the fore again. It is also said *"to hug the cactus"* which means accept the outcome, forgive and adapt. I had a Boss who would harangue people in the most disparaging way and then an hour later was a fine colleague sharing a joke. He had made his point, his way, then forgiven the staff member for making the error and moved on. People of character accept the criticism and appreciate the other person for pointing out where they went wrong. Then somehow, they too are free and move on without taking offence. **Free is the important word here, if you harbor resentment or ill feeling you are diminishing your growth, imposing a sort of weight on yourself, and slowing your path to happiness.** Confucius said, *"he who seeks revenge first dig two graves."* **Be someone who sees every opportunity to forgive as what it is disguised as - an opportunity to grow.** So always be the first to say, *"I accept and forgive you, let's move on together."*

"The first to apologise is the bravest, the first to forgive is the strongest, the first to forget is the happiest." – Ralph Smart

In my Rugby days we had an expression which I personally had many opportunities to learn well, it summed up how to respond to being dropped from the team or being replaced at half time or being stomped on in a ruck by an over vigorous player from your own team! It was – *"Cop it sweet."* It is a good phrase to apply to much in life, just accept any set back with a smile and cop it sweet.

Ironically at the Surf Club too if you were unfairly given toilet cleaning again or dishwashing duties or a double patrol because on the beach you failed to keep eyes, *"out to sea"*, you copped it sweet. One could always go to Owen the club captain. who would sit you down, graciously listen to your complaint about how wrong and unfair this is, he would ask if you felt better now you have pleaded your case? Then ever so nicely say, *"OK you have had your little bleat – now piss off and get on with your penalty!"* A bit like the western movies when the town Sheriff says, *"Son, we will give you a perfectly fair trial and then a perfectly fair hanging."*

So, when you feel you are hard done by just have a laugh, wear it and **cop it sweet. The message is**

important – as a young man or woman take the criticism and in doing so watch yourself change and win respect.

In business when I used to take on a new project my first action was to learn the product inside out and back to front so my product knowledge was first class, then with a captive colleague (a work mate) role play situations. If you can, first role play any presentation with a friend. Many people are terrified of this type of training but be demanding of yourself and with your friend already knowing and of course asking the tough questions this greatly improved my presentation skills. Toastmasters is a fine organisation to overcome fear of public speaking and a lot of fun! By practicing one would become competent and now you should know - confident too! **Then quietly enthusiastic hoping for a positive outcome through negative acceptance. Which means provided I gave this presentation / examination my absolute best, if I lose, I can live with that loss and yes – cop it sweet. This attitude gives one a nice sense of balance in accepting outcomes.** Mind you, no one likes losing but if I do the person who beat me knows they sure did earn it and mostly that person who beat me, in hindsight was usually me! **Due to lack of preparation.**

The great American President Abraham Lincoln stated, *"Give me six hours to chop down a tree, I will spend the first four sharpening my axe."* His analogy of course was preparation. Excellent advice for meeting challenges in life and exams. It is also accepted winning is 90% in the preparation. **Now please remember the six P's – Prior Preparation and Planning Prevents Poor Performance. Or as the great Chinese military leader Sun Tzu said,** *"Every battle is won before it is ever fought."* So, the key to meet challenges is in your preparation, the big games in life are won not so much on the day but in those hard training / study sessions when you are tired and exhausted and you push yourself into areas you never knew existed. I remember Laurie Lawrence the great Australian swimming coach and Australian Rugby player once said to me, *"The pain of a hard training session only lasts a few moments, the pain of defeat can last a lifetime."*

I wholeheartedly agree that ninety per cent of the time we come up short is due to lack of preparation.

I also learned to always follow up with the Lecturer or Coach or Client or Manager after any setback or loss and ask them to help me by requesting, *"Where did I go wrong?"* Then you may find the truthful answer and learn some valuable information.

The wonderful era we live in now gives females more opportunity to discover and maximise their potential. In fact, there is a change in the balance of the world happening right now. An entire range of studies are revealing, the ratio of women to men graduating into Universities and Trades is growing rapidly. Females are performing with higher scores, producing better quality workmanship and becoming more effective leaders across all aspects of society. In recent times women are proving to be better prepared in this more diverse twenty first century. According to the Australian Bureau of Statistics as of May 2021, 55% of enrolled students in universities were female. 50% of the young women in Australia aged from 25-34 now hold a bachelor's degree or above and 85% who successfully completed university studies were employed. In Australia of the 42 Universities 35 had fewer males and two had over 70% females. I understand some

Universities have a bias toward some gender orientated subjects however this closing gender gap is a worldwide phenomenon with the OECD reporting women now account for 56 percent of students enrolled in higher education.

May I ask a question? In your family who is the last person to go to bed every night and the first person up every morning? Mum? Yes, the woman and that holds true the world over in all societies. If an alien race visited us, saw our daily life, and identified the ones who ceaselessly contributed, worked whilst nurturing and raising a family and delivered new life who do you think they would conclude were the Leaders?

The principal of a school in NZ was talking to a Judge about teenagers who said, *"I do not know what to do with these teens, where we can go!"* The Judge responded, *"My answer to this is go home mow the lawn, clean the windows, learn to cook, go fishing, visit the old persons home, study your lessons and after that, pick up a book. The world does not owe you a living, your parents do not owe you fun. In other words, grow up, stop being a crybaby, get out of your dreams and develop a backbone instead of a wishbone. You are important and you are needed. It is too late to sit and wait around for somebody to do something someday. Someday is now and somebody is YOU!"*

My wife used to say to me when I would come home confronted with a mini crisis. *"Ha! We laugh in the face of adversity!"* **In fact, the best natural tonic known to science to confront and reduce anxiety, pressure and anger is LAUGHTER.** My wife's simple comment always drew a laugh and every time renewed my spirits. That is the sort of spirit we are seeking from you. We all must understand every successful person in any field handles pressure well and stays in control. **Never ever lose control.**

Now a most critical point, many times you will enrol on a course or sit an exam or start an exercise or a new task of some sort for example first learning the fine art of playing one bongo! And you want to just quit as it is too hard or boring or not what you thought - **please do not under any circumstances not complete the task.** The benefits will be lifelong.

Quitting gets easier all the time and it is highly contagious!

Future employers look for those who have seen jobs through to completion and view with concern the ones with the half-done courses. The uncompleted course is making a statement about you and your ability to finish tasks. I want you to be an achiever and a leader. **Please note, achievers always finish, even if they fall over the line.** This is so vital in your life, accept the difficulty, you have skin in the game, so keep going even if it takes longer than anticipated and see it through to completion. Please just finish the task no matter how much time it takes. Surveys by top employment firms have proven they are not seeking the smartest or most qualified personnel anymore but the people who quietly persist despite setbacks, the ones with what is called grit and a never give up attitude.

The Japanese have a wonderful culture, a component involves an idea called *Kintsugi.* Sometime in the fifteenth century the artisans would make beautiful pitchers and vases but they were delicate, would often break and then be thrown away. But someone came up with the idea of restoring the items by gluing the pieces back together but with one important component added, gold dust! This became accepted and in fact made the vases even more precious. The same with us. **We all fail and make mistakes, suffer at the hands of others but in accepting our own errors and those of others inflicted upon us and learning from the experience, we can become better even stronger people in the broken places.** Including our ability to build friendships as we now understand the plights of others. This is the Japanese way. **Kintsugi upon you!**

Some of you may just want to be a Peta or Peter Pan and say these instructions are just too hard. I expect this, some will forget through lack of re-reading the advice. But that too is OK because over time you will find your own path, but please promise me one thing during your journey – **On every task, you will never give up, you will finish, whatever it takes! As the only time you will fail is when you stop trying!**

NOTE: There are four key skills to be learned and practiced in the last four chapters, which will be the foundation of the growth in your good self. Do you think you could list them below?

1...

2...

3..

4..

Summary:

- I know the challenges are coming and I accept this as part of life. I will laugh in the face of adversity. When under pressure I will just have a good laugh.

- I know too I will not see them coming! Will I stand up with my head up or will I give up?

- If I lose in some instances, I will learn the lesson I am being shown, accept the loss with grace and move on – *cop it sweet.*

- Facing it, that is the way, always facing it – quitting gets easier.

- I am having a few problems this week but I am not worried because I will have a whole new set next week!

- I will ask myself what is the worst possible outcome here? if I can accept that with humility, I know I will then be OK.

- If I am in error, I will be the first to apologise. I never lose control.

- I will never be caught short through lack of preparation PPPPP- prior preparation and planning prevents poor performance.

- When I feel pressure. I am never found wanting. Every successful person knows they can stand the heat in the kitchen if they will it.

- Through saying no to alcohol and drugs I am growing much faster as I experience life in its realness.

- *"Success is repeatedly failing and not losing any enthusiasm" –WC.*

- Kintsugi - broken and even better.

- I will always complete the task no matter what I will always finish.

- When life opens you up what will it find inside?

- Why me? No TRY ME!

ACTION PLAN:

I need to accept life will challenge me so I can expect those difficulties and prepare myself by the following actions:

1...
....

2...
....

3...
....

4...
....

Which of these options would be my best choice now?

CHAPTER 5

FRIENDS FOR LIFE

"The people who care about you tell you what you do not want to hear and what no one else will."

Oscar Wilde said, *"Some cause happiness wherever they go, others whenever they go."* Afghanistan. I had teamed up in Kabul with what could only be called *a "soldier of fortune"*. He was ex royal navy, XXX large, laconic and tough. His pants were a bit like him, made of some coarse material, hand sewn with leather patches and he could tie a Slippery Hitch and a Sheepshank in a few seconds - specialty being a perfect, thirteen looped noose. Around his neck he wore a red handkerchief, over that the travellers Moroccan *"goolamie"* beads and to top it all off dangling off his chest a huge necklace made of various animal teeth and shells. The strides were held up by a large leather belt, on the buckle were some strange Sanskrit hieroglyphics. Tied to his belt was a huge Kurki knife (the unique weapon of the famous Gurkhas from Nepal to the far northeast). Unlike my machete designed for slashing through ripe watermelons, a Kukri was a thick boomerang shaped honed steel instrument perfectly designed for slashing through throats. His coat if you could call it that was cross stitched as only a sailor knows how. It was made from the fleece of a Yak who inhabit the lands from Siberia to the Himalayas and it fitted him like a labrador fits into a car. He even let go sometimes with a wild barking laugh which would make an Afghan war lord think twice.

Stan had sailed and trekked the globe and been to every place in the world I could throw at him saying, *"Just doing the best I can – son."* Right now, one could not think of a more desolate place on the planet than Chicken Street, Kabul to, *"Do the best I can."* As we travelled together, I concluded he was the freest man I had ever met, but also fitted into the *"mad, bad and dangerous to know,"* category. One day he started whittling a tree branch down to a heavy, long, what I would call a *"waddy"* or in Ireland a *"shillelagh"* or in South Africa a *"knobkerrie."* I queried him and he said, *"That my little Aussie mate is a Boy Stick."* Sure enough soon as we passed through the Khyber Pass and into Pakistan, we were under siege by organised teams of raggedy street kids literally tearing into us for anything they could strip us of, all the while screeching, *"Bakhsheesh"* (a gift). In an instant Stan was out with his boy stick and with a crack on the head, jab in the stomach, whack on the arm or stomp on the toes he gave these larrikins some curry of a different kind. Stan certainly saved our meagre possessions. I made three of these handy items in a range of sizes!

In Delhi after more eye-opening adventures this big jovial wanderer told me we were heading as always towards the rising sun. I enquired as to our destination. Stan responded, *"To the heart of darkness mate!"* Thinking of Christmas in the *"black hole of Calcutta"* sometimes you just sort of know a wonderful friendship is not going to end well, so I was learning sometimes to get out – quick. I knew Stan could quite easily be my undoing and immediately told him I was trekking north. Where to? Well anywhere – in fact. Turned out to be Kashmir about as far north as I could get without worrying about wandering Yeti's of another type!

Friends are serious business. One of the most respected and wealthiest people in the world Warren Buffett said. *"There is nothing more important in life than investing in yourself and who you choose to call your friend."*

My father held up his hand, spread his fingers and said to me, *"Son, in your whole life, if you can fill one hand with true friends, then you will have truly succeeded."* Just watch when someone you know fails badly or makes a significant error of judgement and loses the respect of their peers. See how their friends seem to fall away. We ALL make mistakes we regret, we all *"stuff up"* and the comforting soul of a genuine friend, in those times, is worth their weight in gold.

Back to my Dad's comment of five lifetime devoted friends, averaged out over your lifetime, say you make one rock solid friend every fifteen years. If you leave school with just one person you can rely on and call a best friend and tell them so, you will be well on your way. Please do this for yourself, at least find one and keep in touch with that one, as you two will need each other. **If you are having a rough day, who would you call? You need someone.** "Billie would you mind if I gave you a call when I just need to have a chat? I don't want you to solve my problem." I guarantee this will prove invaluable to you. So how do we go about finding these friends?

Allow me to ask, why would you like someone else or they like you? **One of the major reasons is either you or they see something lacking in themselves and want to be closer to that person and we want to learn what it is.** As to why we do this unconsciously, later we will be unpacking the reason. Conversely, we are always only one bad friend away from having some serious problems. As mentioned, the great Dale Carnegie said, *"Everyone wants to feel important. If you want to be interesting, be interested."* We now show genuine interest in others every time we meet someone. You will find if you keep asking questions about someone's life, everyone has a story to tell even though they may be only fifteen. If we make the effort and challenge ourselves, the more we give in commitment, work, friendship, and kindness the more we seem to receive and the better we feel and enjoy our lives and the company of those around us. The power of the universe at work? Life is so funny as **the best way to make yourself happier is – to do something for someone else.** A simple act of love. *"Shine a light,"* was an expression that Barack Obama (ex-President of the USA) encouraged amongst his staff. This means place the light on another person, recognise their achievements and encourage them when they are down.

For example, ask others and have a bit of fun with these questions:

What is one thing you would want older generations to know about us teenagers today?
The zombie apocalypse is coming, who are three people you want on your team and why?
What is the best piece of advice you have ever been given?
What has scared you more than anything in life so far and how did it happen?
What really interests you as a career if everything possible was on the table and why?
What do you think may be the biggest challenges we face growing up?
What sort of person do you think a real friend should be like?

All these questions are what is called, *"open ended"* which means they require more than a yes or no answer. This is a clever way to engage and open conversations and establish rapport. Be discerning now with your time, search out a genuine, authentic person with similar values to yourself or even more strict, whom you would like to call your friend. Then start developing a relationship both of you could carry forward. Now, this is the important part, when you leave school commit to a quarterly meet up at the latest. **You will need each other more than you ever believed!** You could even form a small circle of best friends and do it that way, though it will be hard for say three or four to catch up and maintain contact on a consistent basis. When soldiers the world over, after going to war, are interviewed and asked the question, *"Why did you endure and fight?"* The soldiers initially respond in the same way by saying either, *"It was our job"* or *"We fought for our country,"* but when probed the genuine answer to the question is always – *"In truth, out there, we fought for each other."*

"A real friend is one who walks in when the rest of the world walks out" – Walter Winchell. **Friends work things out together, they volunteer to help each other out. The people who care about you tell you what you do not want to hear. Do you want to know the secret to living a long and happy life? Keeping your mates alive!** In other words, you be the one who reaches out and you will be rewarded.

There was a mock team building test based on a division of the Canadian Parachute Rescue Squadron. An airplane crashes in the snowy, northwest wilderness and the survivors, to help them stay alive, must select in priority order a number of items from one to fifteen e.g., compass, box of matches, aircraft tyre inner tube, 6m x 6m canvas tarpaulin, book on celestial navigation, 250ml of rum, hand axe, 75 metres of rope, sleeping bag per person etcetera. Each person is asked to number from most important to least important for their survival. Then you break into groups of three or four and collectively pooling their thoughts the participants repeat the same exercise. In every case I facilitated, based on the individual's selections 90% of the participants died or were in critical condition. But when working as a group, they all survived. **Friends can really be life savers.** Many of the best friendships are forged in the crucible of competition or some form of adversity. The finest examples come from the field of conflict, which is war. Gallipoli for example where the spirit of the ANZAC soldiers was born and still thrives to this day. Edward Lynch in his seminal autobiography, *Somme Mud* is an authentic example. Lynch's horrific story of soldiers' front-line experiences in the trenches is a fine example of the hell that was World War One. Lynch finishes his book with the final paragraph which applies to all of us. *"The brightest memory of the war is that I have known real men. Men with the cover off. Men with that wonderful nobility of character, of mateship, revealed. It is a glorious memory to have. To have known men as men. That is something that does not come to everyone. The war is over. The trial was long and severe. The price was worth it though, when measured in the mateship of men. My mates! Memories of men! Memories of mates! Men who were mates and mates who were men."* Friends of all genders are vital to us all.

Some of the best times of my life have been with the odd man out. Strange but a good friend who was something of a philanthropic *"soldier of fortune"* retained me to search for the legendary Lasseters Reef. A starving miner 100 years earlier, Harold Lasseter had stumbled into Port Hedland carrying in his pockets some of the highest gold bearing ore ever found. He said he had discovered an enormous quartz reef kilometres long out in the *"Never Never "* of central Australia. At this time Australia was suffering the ravages of the Great Depression. This "find" could turn the tables! An expedition was launched by a syndicate of businessmen to ostensibly turn our economy around. Bogged, lost, deserted and calling Lasseter a charlatan the adventurers eventually packed it in. However Lasseter ventured on alone determined to prove them wrong, dying in the attempt. My commission was firstly to read all the available literature. Then with an acute case of *"gold fever"* I had to try to re find this reef and was introduced to my partner, leader, tracker and sidekick. A wizened old digger called, would you believe, Joe Strange. Who over many years had ferreted around the bottom of hundreds of derelict old mining shafts! He was laconic, spoke few words had a very lived in face, battered bushie hat and always wore an unfolded long sleeve shirt. On shaking hands I discovered why and was met with a genuine steel hook for a right hand! His bushman skills were amazing and the hook came in very handy picking up a hot tea bucket. NNE of Warburton where the local aboriginal kids butcher and eat barely singed 'Roo and mostly have broken noses from sniffing petrol out of jam tins. We headed south east off the dirt corrugations of the abandoned and suitably named Gunbarrell Highway on a compass bearing. Over countless hills and gullies I sometimes wondered what if out here we did find the *"mother lode"* of world wide gold deposits. After all, two can keep a secret if one is dead!

Camping in the sand dune country of the great silence. Burning the spinifex around us to scare away any inland taipans, centipedes, red backs and paralysis ticks, we pushed on day after day scanning the horizon for Lasseter's geographical signposts in his Diary. Yes we found three hills that may have been, *"the three sisters"* and an amazing quartz reef rising a couple of metres off the earth that actually ran in the stated

NNW/SSE direction but unfortunately or perhaps fortunately, not Lasseters reef of gold. In hindsight a fascinating trip and as for Joe he was a mighty fine fella.

The quietest people are often the ones with a cutting-edge sense of humour. Having met many people of different heritages and cultures I eventually learned the guy with the Mohawk haircut, tattoos, earrings and studs may very well be a fascinating person and staunch friend or all show. Either way never assume based on physical appearance. There are some zany, lovable people out there. When you meet someone new **question and listen with respect** and keep all your options open. Every day is an opportunity for you to practice an important relationship building skill. The fine art of **thinking for a moment - before you open your mouth or act is crucial**. If you respond to anyone in a nasty way with ugly words this will come back to you with vengeance in one form or another. Indeed, many times you could be deliberately provoked to see how you react. This skill is so difficult I still struggle with it, as a natural response is to react in a similar way to a verbal barrage or one word thrown like a slap at you which can never be retracted. Here a smile and a thank you works wonders. The benefits of this skill by being a nice person in building friendships and goodwill are beyond measure. **Unless you have something good to say about someone else – please shut up. The selection of who you choose to be best friends is one of the most difficult tasks you will ever have and one of the most worthwhile. If you want to be liked, be likeable and be authentic.** Friendship can also be manifested by kindred spirits when one person says to another. *"What! You too? I thought that no one but myself...."* — *C.S. Lewis*. If you feel like you are different or weird believe me others feel exactly the same but they are keeping their differences to themselves too. The one or few who become friends for life, those who walk alongside you on this journey will be like lighthouses in the bleak times of fog and darkness and only a phone call away. Please do not consider just your own gender, whoever you respect or even admire is a top candidate and you will never ever know if you never ever go and ask. Good friends come in all shapes and sizes and may have some funny quirks too, like one I know very well who fidgets all the time, knees pumping like a piston and every third word is a four letter one! Of course, some people can be great fun as acquaintances but not necessarily great friends. Some of your friends now may not be included in the next chapter of your book of life. You may already have a good idea who they are. There was a young man who was called, *"the Prince of Perth."* He was one of the most talented footballers in the history of AFL some say the best. Sadly, he teamed up with questionable friends. In one instance on national television, he was seen scampering over roof tops trying to avoid police arrest. His reputation as a prince in tatters. If this man chooses, he could learn the lessons from the experience, put it in the past not allow himself to become a prisoner and again become a champion. Even the absolute best of us can be brought down by the wrong decisions with so called *friends*.

Consider the fable of the scorpion who wants to cross the river, but a scorpion cannot swim so it asks a frog if it can ride on its back. The frog says, *"But you are a scorpion and you will sting and kill me."* The scorpion responds, *"No why would I do that as I cannot swim and if I sting you then we both would die?"* The frog accepts this logic and takes the scorpion on its back, halfway across the frog feels a mighty sting between its shoulders and says, *"No! Why have you stung me now both of us will drown?"* The scorpion replies, *"I do not know why - that is just the way I am."* Some people are charming yet dangerous, why they are like this is rooted somewhere deep in their psyche, be mindful of these personalities and be aware. I have seen many good people drawn into toxic relationships thinking they will be fine and finding themselves in real trouble. *"If you lie down with dogs you will get up with fleas."* **Please remember this: Show me your friends and I will show you who you are and your future!** One can ascertain a good idea of someone's calibre by who they are associating with. You are seeking friends for all seasons that is in good and tough times, the best friends have *"stickability."* **Trust is granted to someone as a solemn promise.** It is earned over time and is the cornerstone of every strong relationship. Hard to gain and valued as the best there is of and in us. If trust is lost and it is easy to do so, it takes years to earn it back, sometimes never. **Cherish this word and if you are considered trustworthy the words speak for themselves as the highest possible recommendation from one to another.** Even when you are no longer friends with someone the secrets they may have shared with you need to be respected. That is a definition of integrity. It is odd too, how sometimes friendships can rekindle and flourish after time as you eventually understand and forgive. Let us have a look at the counter point. The Bully phenomenon. Studies have revealed 50% of 15–17-year-olds are being cyber bullied. No one who is really confident and happy is unkind to others. If someone is mean that is because someone or something has previously frightened them. You may wish to consider the responses below as they work.

1. Look at them or type back and respond with a comment I have used and had a good laugh about, *"You may very well say that however I could not possibly comment".* Or *"R U OK?"* or *"Who hurt you?"* You see hurt people hurt people. If you want an edge to win someone to your way of thinking in a situation say, *"I take your point but I need some help here, can you please explain further OR at a certain level I totally agree."*
2. Just say or type *"Very Good"* and walk away.
3. Ideally if outside a friend will be around **and only needs to stand beside you.**

4. If confronted by a bully, step back, face them, look right in the eye and smile. Say, *"OK I heard you, yes some of what you say is true and walk away"*.

5. Find something nice to say to them like, *"You know what, I have always admired you for this reason- popularity, sports ability, cool gear you wear etc."*

This is called emotional intelligence. If you are respectfully honest that will disarm them every time. By engaging the other party and being genuine, they will more than likely reach out to you as these people certainly need friends. If the aggressor keeps coming, face them and shout out as loud as you can **"STOP!"** If they persist place both hands open and arms stretched out front and say, *"If you touch me forcibly in any way, without my consent that is assault."* If not then RUN!

It has been said, *"if you want to live to 100 then look after your friends."* Let us think about that statement. To me it means by giving of yourself and reaching out you are bringing peace to your own soul and many times a good laugh about times gone by. As well the relationship grows and good friends are a priceless commodity in tough times if only just to listen. **Unfortunately, at the end of the day you will also learn 99% of people you** meet who may be occasional friends or acquaintances or work associates or members of a club or a team, really do not give a *"flip"* about you despite whatever they say and when situations go wrong - they will not be there for you. Realise this, accept it and remember the theory of a positive outcome through negative acceptance. If you expect to be disappointed, then when you are you will not be too surprised. **Family and the handful of friends you are building from now is all you will ever have and then only if you continually work at it.** So, what is the **IT** factor these friends we are looking for must possess to become friends for life?

Summary:

- I will start seeking and developing five friends for life perhaps beginning with a school friend.

- These people will share common values.

- I will follow up with *"quarterly catch ups"* and build on these relationships.

- Good friends are like gold. I will value, cherish, and respect them.

- I always stop and think before responding to any aggressive or insulting or accusatory comments. I never verbally react in anger I delay. I keep any negative opinions about anyone else to myself. I am non judgemental.

- Show me your friends and I will show you who you are and your future. I will be mindful of who I choose to mix with even as acquaintances as this reflects my character.

- *"If you lie down with dogs you will get up with fleas."*

ACTION PLAN:

I need to start determining who my BFF's will be going forward now and after my school days. The ones I pledge to keep in touch with and meet with no matter what happens, this is my promise. Even the person I have always felt could be a good friend, but I never let it be known. I will be upfront and honest and prepare to be surprised as sure as a faint heart never won the day, fortune favours the brave.

These are some possibilities:

1...

2...

3...

4...

CHAPTER 6

IT'S AN INSIDE JOB

"If a lion could speak, we could not understand a word it would say"- Wittgenstein.

Twenty-one, alone on the road. For some curious reason still unbeknown to me, in Genoa Italy I started climbing the massive wall of an ancient beachside castle. After around thirty minutes I found myself halfway up a vertical stone block rampart scared to death and trapped with the glittering Mediterranean a hundred metres below. No way out but to cling like a cockroach. Praying this was not really me, I was even unable to slap some sense into myself. Like an Emu impossible to move backwards, no option but to keep going. A crowd of tourists had gathered on the beach below and others gawking and dripping ice cream on me from above. Not sure if it was a performance from a master Alpinist or the village idiot. An hour later as the beautiful sun set, sweat through, I finally crawled over the top like a drowned cat. Most of the tourists had their amusement for the day and had already departed. I dropped down onto the inside wall-walk exhausted and elated I had made it and survived. Then with the ounce of pride I had left, I jumped up, peered back over the rampart admiring the vista, pretending I was another onlooker looking for me! Then strolled down the hill to the back of the Ristorante plonked against a safer wall on the dirt, With the only ones not amused, the restaurant chooks. I was still in shock thinking, *what was I thinking!*

How is it some of us seem to inherently know to put their best foot forward? Have you ever been told, *"You just don't get it."* I know the expression extremely well! I mean how could I not get it when I already knew everything? You could say I was quite privileged in the school I attended from Year 5 to 12. You could also call it an exclusive boy's only bastion of towering old red brick buildings and grand verandas. Set on twenty-one hectares or fifty-two prime acres of city real estate truncated by a great moat, really a creek. The whole place was like some ancient fiefdom.

My school produced champion athletes, swimmers, footballers, doctors, lawyers and even several Rhodes scholars. All under a cult of competition which through some sort of osmosis it was expected we would all leave the citadel as incarnations of high achievement. But for some reason I never made, "*the cut.*" I wanted more than anything to fit in and be accepted. A bit lonely mostly and overthinking everything. I was totally missing the focus of this fine school which was delivering the best possible education available. I commenced Prep. School with averages in the 70% plus range and proceeded to drop down in scores and in classes annually from 3A in Year 5 to 6F in Year 12. I worked hard at becoming popular, for all the wrong reasons. Daydreaming in class, running down the curriculum, as to my conceited mind algorithms were of no practical application. And kidding around all the time and I mean being a kid. Not a person to earn respect and be respected, a lightweight, never a part of the focussed cohort who got **IT**.

I became a bit of a knockabout who never had the epiphany of situational awareness bestowed. A go along for the ride type or a NAV (no added value). One of the boys who mixed it up with the Boarders (students who lived in). It seemed to me that all the Boarders came from fabulous, *"Stations"* out in the bush and were immediately identifiable by their odd kangaroo hide plaited belts bound with two steel rings in the front. Each one of them was bush hard, possessing what I found a remarkable trait in that these guys simply would never give up. In hindsight the one thing that may have subliminally rubbed off on me. Sometimes at school holiday time their parents would pick them up in a flash, expensive car and a couple of times their Dad arrived midterm in the beaten-up farm Ute. My mates taken back home to help kill their own starving stock. Such was life in the bush. These country folk all seemed to have already done way more living than us, *"day boys."* Their academic care factor at school was generally a bit below par because most were just going back to the farm to carry on what they had been doing with Dad and him with his Dad for generations. These were the men who would eventually take over *"the sunlit plains extended"* of the family cattle or sheep station.

I was a Day Boy or a *"greaser"* which I still think meant when the final bell rang, we were gone out the gate like grease on a rail. However, I got on well with these *"salt of the earth bushie"* types. In Year 12 when asked by my Form Teacher Mr. Smith who coincidentally taught me in Year 5 as well (so he saw from Prep. to Middle and Senior school, my whole *"old school tie"* education) what I wanted to do for a career? I said, *"go bush and become a jackaroo."* A jackaroo or jillaroo is a trainee, *"roustabout"* or what some call a *"useful."* The most basic job for someone with no skills who really needs to find out what they are made of. I remember Mr. Smith on hearing my response paused and turned to look out the window past the Great Hall and on over the expansive playing fields. He sat there staring for quite a while, seemingly lost in silent contemplation......

I must admit somewhere along the way of my education at this most prestigious school which, with two other brothers also attending, must have cost my battling parents a small fortune, I started to treat school as somewhere to well, fill in the time. You could say I put the less into hopeless! I wanted to be liked and made myself the fool to buy friendships and sacrificed an education. So perhaps it was not too surprising that I used to really enjoy the company of the knockabout boarders! I knew exactly the pathway I had chosen, one of the inconsiderate and contemptuous. And in doing so my school passport was stamped as a person of no value and no values. Allow me to request that you be tolerant whilst I give you one example of my developing character, which to this day I am still ashamed.

Talking in our daily chapel service earned a severe penalty by way of *"five of the best"* from a Lawyer Cane, a 1.2 metre length of Australian cane cut from the stand-alone sentinel down near the Navy cadets building. Which was the best maintained and manicured home-grown school plant in twenty-one hectares!

Speaking in chapel was banned. Feeling particularly robust one day I chose to endear myself to a newly promoted Prefect two years my senior seated in the pew behind me. So, I casually leaned back and told him he was an oxygen stealing *"buggerlug"* and a *"cross country wrestler"* to boot! The recipient of my observation was also Head of the Debating Team and destined to be a top-class Attorney at Law. He gave me a curious look then nodded in assent to my comment. At precisely 09:50 moments before Morning Tea, I was summoned from the classroom to attend the office of the Deputy Headmaster, whose nickname was *"Bat."* As he would often be seen flying down the cloisters in his black cape. I duly attended his office, whereupon Bat clearly elucidated my misdemeanour. Then concluded by informing me of the extraordinary fact that I would thank him for this caning and it was going to hurt him more than it was going to hurt me! I was told to touch my toes whilst he eyed me up and down and chose his weapon of choice from an eye watering array of canes beside his filing cabinet. After the initial obligatory tap, tap, tap on my rear to make sure I was sweating, the Bat swung into action with as was called, *"five of the best"*. At lunch time, there he was, my nemesis, gliding down the cloisters looking aloof, a dip and a quick shoulder and straight into the hat rack. That afternoon, between periods, my rage had to be vented, so the old *"sleeper hold"* seemed the only solution. By day's end due to my penchant for retribution I had attended Bat's office twice more and received ten more "cuts" on the behind!

I hobbled home from school at 3.15pm being waved goodbye by the Boarders applauding with thanks for the entertainment. As regards to the Prefect, his silence throughout the misdemeanour and through to his matriculation still unnerves me. In relation to thanking the Bat for the caning, that matter still remains unresolved.

Despite my best efforts I always made the Swimming Squad but never the Swimming Team. I made the Athletics Squad but never the Athletics Team. In football however I made the Rugby Third Fifteen! To this day I regret my apathy and willingness to learn the lessons, an opportunity lost.

Why could I not see the lesson being taught over and over in one eight-hour day? I could have easily turned the whole situation in my favour. Firstly, followed the rules and never spoke in chapel or sincerely apologised. Then volunteered to take the initial punishment and earn some respect from the Prefect and the Master. As I later learned to do so many times over the years it would have been a far better option if I had welcomed many problems as opportunities to gain respect by admitting wrongs and growing up.

Interestingly none of the boat crew members were ever hauled up before the school hierarchy. In fact, most of them already held school appointments in one way or another or were on the way to recognition.

Perhaps we could dig a bit deeper into this mysterious world of a sport where you face backwards to go forwards. There is a saying, *"real athletes' row, the rest just play games."* At our school I remember these curious car bumper stickers saying, **"Rowing builds Character."** I used to wonder what that was all about. In hindsight one of my few great regrets in life is that I never took up the challenge of rowing when I was younger. So how does, *"pushing a puddle"* fast track one's character? Once on the inside of a boat shed wall, I saw a message written, *"If I pass out, please note my time."* What madness is that? Imagine a sport so pure there is no physical contact of any kind or any ball to kick or stick to throw or bar to jump? It seems it is just you against you and a few others along for the ride. Those along with you who never say a word and yet make it impossible for you to say, *"I'm out of here!"*

A boat race is defined as, *"A journey into hell over 2000 metres in eight lanes,"* Each person must be able, upon request, to call upon the absolute fury of the *"berserker,"* but remain in total controlled form, sitting in a tiny, shiny shell about as wide as their butt and a hand's width from the water. Rowing demands the very best qualities in all of us. Iron discipline, total commitment, integrity, friendship at its finest without saying a word with a will and purity of form that only is achieved when the whole crew is acting in perfect unison. And I am told when the vessel seems to move entirely of its own volition, tiny bubbles can be heard flowing under the boat! Rowers usually maintain the beauty and solace with the silent timing and grace of the rowing experience on the water at dawn and dusk. Serendipity. My wife took it up in her "fifties" and discovered this wonder. You may wish to team up with a friend, even start with surf boats, meet and become one of these quiet remarkable people of character. **Whatever, join a club outside of school.**

I am humbled to say that the connections and friendships I developed from that great school have been a blessing for which I am grateful to this day. I only wish I had understood **IT** and acted upon the wonderful opportunity my long-suffering parents had given me at the time.

At school in hindsight my thinking process was underdeveloped and I was singularly immature. I just could not see **IT** and **IT is an inside job IT is totally up to you!**

One could say you have two minds, one that ceaselessly interrupts you with stressful *"what if's"* and another, **the Observer**. Eckhart Tolle's great book, The Power of Now explains this as the *"self"* and the *"pain body"*. The Ego or your own pride. **Do not let a past or future event turn into thinking about it. Stay the Observer. Overthinking the "what if's" can drive you bonkers! THEY ARE ONLY THOUGHTS THEY HAVE NO POWER.** The person who finds peace from disruptive interfering thoughts is the one who sees these thoughts entering their mind and then chooses to see them off. **This is a key life skill, realise when the**

stressful or negative thought is making itself known, recognise it, say OK then push it away out of your thinking. Buddhists call this the *"monkey brain"* which visits us every day, continually chattering away with anxious *"what if's"* which sometimes may even be destructive thoughts and mostly will never even happen. The *monkey brain* is your own ego / pride wanting to take over and be in control.

I should have been clear about what I wanted to achieve. I should have aspired to an exciting productive future by setting my highest standard in everything I did, in and out of the classroom. **Thinking like a person who has a high care factor with purpose and acting like someone who should be regarded as a winner who knew full well that they had been given an incredibly special opportunity**. You see I never got **IT**! My parents had never explained **IT** to me, neither did the Teachers, they just expected me to know **IT**. Some boys knew **IT** and went after **IT** with a will from day one. I am sure you know what I am referring to.

IT = Giving everything you do, everything you have, to help set yourself up to be the best you can be!

If you can give the teachers your total concentration until you become the best you can, do the right thing, have the courage to ask questions when you do not understand, try to sit at the front of the class ALL the time, commit to your homework and study (revise, read or start next tutorial) for two hours each evening Monday-Thursday (forty-five minutes before dinner and ninety minutes afterwards) and stay away from the ones who don't get IT. Pretty much nothing will stop you.

There is a story by Lolly Daskal about four people named Everybody, Somebody, Anybody and Nobody. *There was an important job to be done and Everybody was sure that Somebody would do it. Anybody could have done it, but Nobody did it. Somebody got angry about that, because it was Everybody's job. Everybody thought Anybody could do it, but Nobody realized that Everybody wouldn't do it. It ended up that Everybody blamed Somebody when Nobody did what Anybody could have.* **The message just do it and go from a NAV (no added value) to a GAV (guaranteed added value).**

It was my first day with a national public company and I was tasked with seeing what I could do to win back twenty-five major accounts which had been lost to the opposition. So, I started on the phone. By morning tea, I had *"phonophobia!"* I had to try to keep laughing and for some strange reason I wanted to find a bucket of water and put my head in it! Hung up on, abused, insulted, ranted upon and so many, *"How dare you call us!"* I had the thousand-yard stare! I started to understand how at some companies, new recruits worked to morning tea, went for their break and were never heard or seen again. In retrospect was I being tested? It was curious how the *"gang"* in telephone sales seem to be exchanging five-dollar notes like it was five minutes before race five at the racetrack!

I had to consider other options, so I started turning up at the offices of these ex-major accounts pleading for a few minutes time and then listening with the utmost intent whilst I nodded and took notes. It became evident all these clients had perfectly good reasons for dumping us. But back at head office no one had wanted to admit we had dropped the ball. Fortune favoured me and eighty per cent of these fine organisations returned, since I was offering one particular service. An authentic, high care factor, dedicating myself as their single point of contact across their entire business. That is account enquiries, pickups, deliveries, sales, customer service, ordinance movements, logistics and of course complaints. Many becoming top ten accounts again and a few of the managers valued friends. Plus, I was promoted, I think, at this time I was given another thirty lost clients to win back!

It is interesting to note too, once you commit to giving a task all you have something changes and it no longer seems like work. Often, I was there joking with Pio the night cleaner as he dabbed his vacuum under my feet. But boy did I get some work done without the interruptions. A very successful colleague once said to me, *"Ray it's not hard, this is how I became a partner. Just be in the office every day at 8am and be the last to leave!"* It works. I was also told to never leave my desk empty handed when walking around the office. Grab a file or some papers, tuck them under your arm and stride with purpose. As a bit of a joke, I took this to the extreme and people noticed my dogged commitment, head down with a stoic grim façade loaded up with documents even when heading to the toilet! To the stage where one colleague said, *'Ray slow down mate you are making us all look bad!"* Work can be fun too as we play the game but activity does not mean results. Results means delivering positive, measurable, outcomes. **You are on a journey of finding out what you are really made of and sadly so few of us ever do.**

It is important to somehow arrange an area for you set aside at home to study in privacy. Not that I did that. My designated homework and study location was in the eye of the household storm, our kitchen. That is not what you need. **What you need is your own desk in a quiet spot with a lamp and a good chair.** My wife and I ensured that both our children had a place like this and the improvement in performance was significant with both graduating from university. In creating the best environment, you are setting yourself up for success. To stay focussed you may have to be a bit selfish and explain why and forsake a few others, but so be it. This is because they more than likely as yet, do not get **IT**. **But you get IT because you realise that, right now, you**

are laying down the cornerstones of a success template for the rest of your life.

In business I often noticed, whenever I had a momentous year financially and in other aspects, I had never worked so hard and enjoyed life so much. In any profession your results are a direct reflection of your input. Never a truer word spoken than, *"The harder I work the luckier I get"* – Thomas Jefferson.

The normal labour required is thirty-eight hours through a five-day week. I have met doctors, lawyers, and trades people whose work ethic is up to eighty hours per week, every week. There is nothing surer than in order to make **IT** and really enjoy life there is a direct correlation between time in and results out. Every single top performer in any industry has an overabundance of **IT** and what is more, most seem to love **IT** and the discipline too.

People say find something you are passionate about, and you will never work a day in your life. Well, I still do not know what I am passionate about even now, let alone as a teenager. But I can act passionately doing just about anything if I choose to and that has always delivered for me! The concept of following your passion does not stand up to me. Your passion may be catching butterflies and there is not a significant return wandering meadows with a butterfly net to keep you fed, clothed, and housed. That is unless you catch a few Kaiser I Hind, Emperor of India butterflies. These butterflies for the financially motivated are found flitting around the canopy of the highest treetops, in the most isolated mountain ranges of the Himalayas. Plus, some of us are less motivated by money, some seek fulfilment in service roles which in many ways are just as rewarding.

Bestselling author Mark Manson has said, *"I suggest you define what you feel you are good at, as you are already competent at this action. Then give it everything you have until you become the best you can at it, then you will really be in the game, receive the benefits and simultaneously have become passionate."* Oprah Winfrey said something similar – *"The number one lesson I can offer you is…to become so skilled, so vigilant, so flat-out fantastic at what you do that your talent cannot be dismissed. The point: Become so good you can't be ignored."*

If you become the best, you can at something which there is a demand for and better than virtually anyone else then people will come to you and bring their money too. But highly paid jobs demand long hours and are usually very stressful so you have to ask yourself a question. Will I take and do I want this challenge?

My brother and I used to go out the back of our house every day and kick a football to each other coincidentally for around twenty minutes and continually make it more difficult with small stabbing kicks then low and high passes until our ability to catch a ball seemed natural and we were recognised for this skill level. I learned to do the same with work presentations. It is said if you want to become proficient get some lessons. If you want to become an expert teach yourself.

Personally, I was good at *"bumping the gums"* and convincing others that some of my ideas, like making mosquito coil detonators tied to homemade gunpowder for insertion in our neighbour's letter boxes was not my idea at all! As a result, my career started at rock bottom in sales and what a journey! A vital part of which was role playing. That is difficult as you are trying to persuade your own colleagues of the features and benefits of your product and they know all the objections!

Please google; myfuture.edu.au/bullseyes and jobjumpstart.gov.au to start exploring jobs that relate to the skill set that you already like and are relatively good at.

For example:

- The Defence Force earns you a paid trade or qualification, after two to six years you can depart and enter the corporate world
- I am a good talker - Teacher, Human Resources, Sales
- I love travel - Airline staff, Travel Agent, Border Force, cruise ship staff or crew, Navy
- I like to give of myself and help others – Social Worker, Nursing, Teaching, Policing, Medicine, Dentistry

- I like art and drawing - Architect, Computer graphic designer
- I love music - Programmer, Music engineers, *Bongo player*
- I enjoy the wonder of microscopic objects – Science, Research
- I love reading, writing - Journalism, Publishing, Librarian
- I am fascinated by people - Psychology, Media studies
- Environment fascinates me – Naturalist, Ranger, Plant Nursery
- I love sport – Physiotherapist, Human Movements
- Computers excite me – Cyber security, Graphic Design, Robotics
- I like coming up with good ideas – Advertising, Marketing, PR
- I am good at making things – Architect, Builder, Designer
- I love the water – Marine Biology, Fisheries, Conservation

- Never disdain the myriad of government roles either, all my friends who ventured down that path and persisted did very well

Mind you out of the gifted and or committed who go on to university, many fail or simply choose to depart. Those who find their niche and complete set themselves up for wonderful careers in high paid fascinating vocations. Plus, on graduation that piece of paper is worth more than gold as it makes a huge statement. Here is a person who is smart, persists to the end and delivers a positive outcome. **Google Open Universities Australia and have some fun with their quiz to see what you may like as a potential career.**

But if peering into a microscope or catching tadpoles is not your cup of tea, then there is a cornucopia of other options which also can deliver big payouts and job satisfaction. The people who are the backbone of this country like the small business owner with the corner hairdressing shop, tradespeople like plumbers and bricklayers (at the time of writing this booklet *"brickies"* were being paid $3.00 to lay a brick and the best can lay 1000 a day!) Even the not so humble salesperson working on commission only, refusing to ever accept a NO for an answer (depending on how many no's they can handle) has an unlimited earning capacity. I know a few of the above category who earn over $1 million a year. I remember being told, this business of selling comes down to one thing, **"making the calls!"** They fail because the rejections eventually defeats them. Again, as Shackleton said, *"those who endure conquer."* Or follow your own path and give of yourself in those personally so rewarding public service roles. **The benefits in all the good things that follow from persisting and being resilient will outweigh all your challenges on the journey.** It comes back to what floats your boat. **But without goals and self-discipline, to put it simply – nothing happens. Think hard on what you are naturally good at, where this skill would work well.** Then add some rocket fuel to your tasks with 100% effort, then passion will follow and you will be unstoppable. You could speak to your parents about helping you with some volunteer work in an area you feel aligned with and do it.

So, whilst you are looking around for the career you would love, if you are not feeling enthusiastic just act like you are, and in doing so you will become so! Because as I have been told, many times, jokingly I hope, *"Ray if you're not fired with enthusiasm, you will be fired with enthusiasm."* Meaning, give everything you have every day with the right attitude. I learned to love the *can-do attitude* and the more commitment required the better I seemed to perform and enjoy my roles. I know some subjects like science can be a little boring but you can choose to be interested. If you say so it will be so. So, act as if it is interesting and you may very well become interested because you are being taught this for a reason, if nothing else to help uncover where your destiny may lie. Plus, it will stop boredom. Make a boring class a game by focussing on the subject matter and committing to taking up to ten relevant notes be the end of the lesson. If you commit to being enthusiastic about everything you do, you will be doing something special – establishing what is called a habit pattern. And once you have that work ethic you never seem to lose it. It does not matter what vocation you take on be it biologist or beautician, soldier or surgeon **you will be used to committing with all you have to the task. That gives you an edge.**

If I can express myself as simply as I can, **the better you do at school the more choices you will have after school. It is not a matter of how smart you are but how much you are prepared to deliver at school to achieve the highest and best results**. Any type of work you may choose whether laying tiles or designing aircraft, life responds in proportion to the effort and your efforts must start now. **Then you are forming a habit of best effort all the time.**

If you want to be a Nurse or a Builder, they are great professions, if you want to go to university or join the Public Service or even become a Jackaroo/Jillaroo would it not be nice to be able to pick any of the aforementioned choices due to your final examination results? Knowing you can choose to do whatever you want whenever you want after you give yourself a little more time to see what is out there. Or just travel until your mind sees **IT** and then go back and choose your career. This is the ideal place to position yourself. So, stop, think and commit to aim for the best possible ATAR or Pathway score you can achieve. You have nothing to lose and a world of possibilities to gain. Because then you can decide which sort of tool you choose to work with a saw, slide rule or scalpel. An exam outcome of 50% average gives you some options, 60% gives you more and 80% starts to open all types of professions and opportunities and then the world can become your *"favourites"* chocolate shop.

But achieving this means giving **IT** everything you have for the balance of high school or the next few years. This will also set you up for success in other areas of life, areas that you do not even know of now - just trust me on this one and DO IT NOW. From now on for the next year or two or three give **IT** everything you have and leave the rest of the guys and girls who are not with you on that quest to make their own arrangements! Becoming this new you, may create some resentment amongst *"friends"* which is OK as it confirms you are committing, and you will be unmoved or indifferent to their attempts to change you back to the old you. Plus, new friends will flow to you, those all with the same sense of determination.

Mix with the girls and boys who are putting in, not the mischief makers. Find those kindred spirits and grow together and lay the foundations for your success.

In fact, as mentioned it is often the girls at this stage who are the most industrious and generally leading the classes. So, align yourself with the winners. Sadly, at my boys only school sharing anything with the attentive, focussed nature of committed young female students was just a faraway concept still full of wonder. You are still the same person but soon **you will have targets to hit and suddenly life will have meaning.** If we achieve something or fix something that gives our lives meaning, be it a relationship or finishing a project. Imagine going through this wonderful journey, looking back and saying to yourself, *"Say what! I did it!"* **Even if you are not in the top few per cent in your class, do not worry, if you can put your hand on your heart and say I gave it my best you will have established a discipline in yourself that you will carry for life**.

Two of the most successful friends I know were from tough neighbourhoods, one a waitress and the other a concreter. They were certainly not what you would call outstanding students, just average folk like anyone you meet, both however I am sure would endorse every piece of advice in this handbook. **The above will require focus so this tip may be of benefit.**

It was discovered by Italian, Francesco Cirillo whilst studying at university he had a kitchen timer on his desk shaped like a pomodoro (tomato). Cirillo noticed an interesting occurrence. After around twenty-five minutes his ability to concentrate wavered. Studies subsequently revealed the maximum time for optimal concentration is around twenty-five minutes, then many of us start to lose focus. **So, every twenty-five minutes you have a *"Pomodoro"*.**

Stretch, move your head, neck shoulders, legs and feet. Then do a 478. Breathe in for four seconds, hold it for seven seconds and slowly but strongly breathe out for eight. If you can, walk around and swing your arms for a few minutes. You mind will love you for it. **This is called "The Pomodoro Technique" proven to revitalise you and help concentration. However, if you are already focussed and, in the zone, - keep going.** There is a wonderful saying by Henry Thoreau, *"If a person does not keep pace with their companions, perhaps it is because they hear a different drummer. Let them step to the music they hear."* Meaning for some, all the trappings of the material world and financial achievement leave them unimpressed. We need those people badly as they are another type of seeker, please note these traits will work for them equally as well. **The message is always the same, just apply these skills to the _"music"_ you hear, and your way will be revealed to you.**

The Road Not Taken by Robert Frost

Two roads diverged in a yellow wood,
And sorry I could not travel both
And be one traveler, long I stood
And looked down one as far as I could
To where it bent in the undergrowth;

Then took the other, as just as fair,
And having perhaps the better claim,
Because it was grassy and wanted wear;
Though as for that the passing there
Had worn them really about the same,

And both that morning equally lay
In leaves no step had trodden black.
Oh, I kept the first for another day!
Yet knowing how way leads on to way,
I doubted if I should ever come back.

I shall be telling this with a sigh
Somewhere ages and ages hence:
Two roads diverged in a wood, and I—
I took the one less travelled by,
And that has made all the difference.

Whichever path you do choose you may be thinking this all sounds just too hard, it is too late or I am not cut out for this sort of challenge, sure that is OK and a normal reaction. However, if you are on board, I suggest you start slowly with purpose on the road less travelled.

One overrider, never allow yourself to become discouraged. If you start to feel that way, get some air and exercise because your old self is trying to make you revert back to the child. Plus, also note discouragement is highly contagious this fable illustrates. The Devil in the marketplace selling his wares. They are all laid out on a table wrapped up in bows and coloured paper with prices attached. Greed, hatred, pride, laziness and so on and one of these packages is twice the size and half the price of all the others and a buyer says, *"What is that one which seems such excellent value?"* The Devil replies, *"Ahhhh that is discouragement, I love selling discouragement because when I do, they always come back and buy all the rest of my products no matter what price I put on them."* I have always found this story most instructive.

When one becomes discouraged you are bound tight with disappointment. We can define disappointment in another form. It is the length of the distance in the diagram following between Expectation and Reality.

What you hope or expect to happen as opposed to what you are prepared to face as reality:

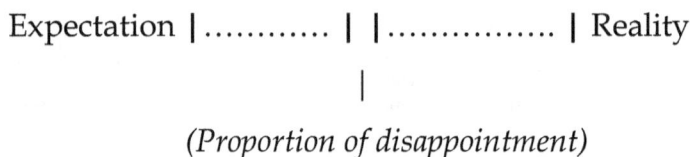

Expectation | .... | | .... | Reality

|

(Proportion of disappointment)

The wider the gap the more disappointed you will be.

You will be disappointed but that means you cared. I found a good way to learn was to say to myself. *"Well, if I give it my best shot and do not make it what happens?"* I could then accept any outcome, learn and carry on. The two hardest things in the world are, *"getting started and never quitting,"* because as we know, **it is always the thinking of the doing not the doing which is the challenging part.** Many of us put off stuff because we do not want to get it wrong. We are not lazy we just want it to be good and we delay. Procrastinators tend towards perfection. Once you have started it is never as hard as you feared, it is the thinking of the act that is the problem, a bit like taking a leap of faith at a school camp. Everyone who jumps for the high rope makes it but 100% of those who do not try do not, as they never gave themselves the chance and just thought themselves out of it. As the great Ice Hockey player Wayne Gretzky said, *"I miss 100% of the shots I never take."*

"I'll have a go," is one of my all-time favourite statements. I love to hear it. **Show me the person who will try and then give their absolute best in everything they do every time and I will show you someone impossible to defeat.** Can we say we have clarity here? From now on will you be enthusiastic about everything you do? If you do not feel it just act it and your mind will follow. **If you want to be lucky your whole life, give everything you do everything you have, that will be enough and your future will fall into place!** No matter what happens just keep trying your best and keep turning up as Woody Allen said, *"80% of success in life will come from just always showing up."*

If you wanted to precis this chapter into two skills only, the actor Will Smith said these two simple actions to get you heading in the right direction, which I can endorse 100%:

1. **Start Running** – when you run you activate your endorphins which create a positive, wellness feeling. Mind, it is impossible to be stressed when you are exercising. Every doctor will tell you laughter and the old *"jig jog"* are the best medicines. Plus, there is a bonus - you will start to push yourself and in doing so you will grow mentally more resilient and physically more robust.

2. **Start Reading** – There have been millions of books written over time. No matter what your concern is or ambition or even how to make the perfect Scone, there is a book about it! Please note I am not referring to the Internet or Chat GPT either which is also called *"potted"* knowledge enabling one to condense everything into summaries. Whereas a book is a *"tree"* with roots and substance. If you become an avid reader the benefits are boundless in your growth as a knowledgeable person and the key to life, success and happiness is knowledge.

So now you get **IT** how do I channel this desire and commitment to achieve and find **IT**? The answer is in the next chapter.

Summary:

- It's an Inside Job! From this day on I am a different person: I act with respect, honour and integrity. I keep my word.

- I get "IT" from now I am going to give everything I do everything I have; I will act with purpose and intent. I am a GAV.

- I associate with triers I talk and act like a humble winner.

- I am going to upgrade my scores in every area and set a target.

- I will always show up: no matter what the *"weather"* I will turn up. Eighty percent of success is just showing up.

- I will have a try at any challenge provided it aligns with my values.

- I will give every task my absolute best then it no longer becomes work.

- My life comprises Running and Reading as essential behaviours.

- If I leave school and do not know what to do then perhaps apply for a job as a Jackaroo /

Jillaroo on an outback Station for six months. Or save a few grand and do the lap of Oz with a friend. Or as I did go for the big one around the planet. This will help find my true self and realise a degree of clarity and purpose. (Look up; Year13.com.au; Gap Year – Google or Ringers From The Top End - rftte.com).

- Join a club or do some volunteer work, great for your CV and others.

- I know to take a Pomodoro break if I can every 25 minutes or just shake out arms legs and neck and do a 478-breathing exercise.

- Download a PDF copy of a very small book, A Message to Garcia. It will take 10 minutes to read and could change your life. It did so for me.

- I will have my own study area with a desk and lamp. I will do forty-five minutes before dinner and ninety minutes afterwards of homework and revision and then nothing will stop me

ACTION PLAN:

What do I need to do to change my attitude and become the best I can? How can I start totally committing to my work, particularly what I am good at perhaps for the first time and in doing so become a person who is known to be dependable, with high standards and actions:

1...
....

2...
....

3...
....

4...
....

CHAPTER 7

THE IMPORTANCE OF SETTING GOALS

"Nothing is ever going to be given to you, everything is going to be earned. If you don't go out there and put in the work, you don't put in the effort, one, you're not "gonna" get the results. But two, more importantly, you don't deserve it". – Tiger Woods

I recall late one night cramped in the third-class carriage of the train leaving the holy city of Benares / Varanasi and curiously the wonderful Indian tolerance of each other was disrupted with people in panic and scattering everywhere. Chooks squawking, goats bleating and the passengers literally climbing over each other to get out of the way as something was entering our carriage. It was not the dreaded ticket collector or some animal escapee smuggled aboard as I initially thought hand on my trusty *"watermelon slicer."* Instead, it appeared to be an upside-down hessian sack, only about a metre high which was sort of gliding down the centre walkway like on one of those airport people movers or a bride with a great train of her dress behind her when she seems to just move of her own accord. The upside-down sack had a ragged hole in it two-thirds of the way up below the corners of the bag where a small, bandaged stump protruded, bound to and around a battered little tin cup. The sound which came wailing out was like a chant I had never heard before, not the infernal *"baksheesh."* This was a cry from ages past, hundreds, thousands of years ago, it was a terribly sad lament. *"Alms sahib alms, alms sahib alms."* The body in the bag was in fact a Leper and whilst I sat transfixed (like when, a few weeks earlier, a massive king cobra had reared up and come at me). Suddenly I had made three, new best friends Ali, Navi and Swami climbing all over me trying to burrow themselves in between me and the back of my wooden bench seat. Imagine the life of this poor soul in the sack whose goal was just to survive another day?

Trust me here. Everybody is trying to just get by. When people used to ask me how I am, I used to quote, *"Just doing the best I can."* Now the important part, the best I can at what?

You have probably owned a dog. Ever noticed *"Spud"* start running around in circles chasing flies or furiously digging holes or chewing the sole off every *"runner"* you leave outside? Sometimes the pooch may even come up and stare at you as if to say – **Well?** What do all these actions mean? **He/she is screaming for a purpose.** Give me something, anything! Our dogs like people can become anxious, depressed and even downright nasty.

When a ship sails out of the port what is the first thing the captain looks at? His maritime charts to the destination. If the captain does not do this the ship will motor aimlessly around in circles, so the captain goes to his charts and plots a course to the port or goal. When the airline flight crew has all the clearances at the end of the runway to become airborne what do they do? The pilot puts the throttle full bore to the floor, not halfway or two-thirds or even 90% but all the way to achieve lift off and then, when up and away throttles back heading towards the designated city. Any less than 100% throttle will result in the plane just taxiing to the end of the runway. **I am asking you now to commit 100% even for**

the first time not 70% or 80%. Everything you have is required and you will fly to your destination.

In fact, you have a vast reservoir of strength inside you which many of us never tap into. It just lies dormant waiting and is sometimes never called upon to respond. You read of people who have suddenly stood up and saved others' lives by single-handedly lifting a vehicle with a trapped child underneath or broken records it was believed could not be broken. Awaken the tiger inside, she sleeps but believe me she lives, only most of us never wake her up!

We are going to lock into place our destination – otherwise our ship just goes round in circles like I used to do at school or back and forth to that office previously mentioned! Steven Covey wrote a world-wide best seller – he studied 150 of the most effective and successful businesspeople and amazingly – all possessed the same seven habits! **Now this is interesting, Covey said the number one habit with every one of those super high achievers was, *"To begin with the end in mind"* which is a goal or an objective or a target.**

So, we can now conclude **IT** needs **you to have a GOAL.**

After I stumbled through Year 12 and entered the workforce, I was a young, brash, even cocky private school rooster who thought I deserved a place at the table of success. By some extraordinary injustice I then managed to get *"freed up"* (political speak for fired) from my first three jobs, a bit like as previously mentioned one of my favourite sayings we all must learn, *"One day a rooster, the next day a feather duster."*

On the overseas trip when I left my mates in London was when my life started to change. I now had to face life alone and treacherous, to find what I was made of or high tail it home. Please bear with me, as I share with you some of my experiences on the journey which became a crash course in going from a *"know all"* to beaten and broken but a goal setter able to endure. There are some attempts at humour other experiences not funny at all. Did the fire of having a purpose set my butt ablaze, please you be the judge:

- Nearly broke in Europe I took to strolling into roadside restaurants full of feigned confidence and

163

casually ordering a free water while taking a strategic table. Where I would remain, stomach growling, waiting for others to finish their meal. Then casually slide over and pile all their leftovers onto one plate and head down, decimate the scraps. Then I'd skulk out like a cowed dog feeling the eyes of other patrons on my neck but offset by the bliss of a full belly. Hungry and ashamed but becoming less so and more resiled to this harder existence.

- Alone in Germany spent one terrifying night in the Black Forest, just down from the crumbling walls of the real Frankenstein's castle. My imagination was running off the scale, I was mesmerized by a moon which had by some osmosis transformed into a giant yellow eye in the sky staring right at me. Convinced it was growing in menace every moment I remember climbing deep into my sleeping bag alone and terrified thinking, *"It's alive, it's alive!"*

  - Solo in central Turkey at dusk with no luck hitching rides. Somewhere near Mt. Ararat I remember walking off the road a hundred metres into a dark, wadi /gully or far enough not to be run over. Put the groundsheet down, rucksack as

164

a pillow and with my trusty machete handy I stared at the stars alone and pretended I was not shaking with fear.

- One day, hungry as always, I was standing in front of a store which featured an array of tasty morsels. Unbeknown to me Turkey produced world class weightlifters and wrestlers. I had another great idea and challenged the manager to an arm-wrestling contest winner gets to eat, loser cleans the kitchen. This caused a bit of entertainment, so he rallied some locals around, shortly after mop in hand he led the way to his preparation area out the back. A mini slaughterhouse covered in blood with the remnants of both dead and soon to be dead, trembling goats.

- Helped drive one of two brand-new Mercedes Benz through to Iran for a wealthy Arab, *"businessman"* with a genuine nose like a hawk and a big silent, moustached, sidekick. I still wonder why they needed a driver. Perhaps my Benz was special? The family turned out to be lovely people, who once in Tehran insisted, I watch slaughter the sacrificial goat. Afterwards whilst my hosts slept blissfully on the roof, I remained totally wide-awake peering into the great Persian sky smiling a grimace of pretended bliss all night. Often thinking about that poor goat, all the blood and wondering if the intestines and head will need mopping up in the morning.

- When lost, somewhere near Kandahar Afghanistan with a friendly *Yank* riding in the back of his VW Kombi we had a run in at some obscure checkpoint with a very dishevelled Afghan soldier who demanded our passports. Whilst he was reading them upside down, my American friend in an unmistakable *"Y'all come"* southern rebel tone demanded back our passports or the wrath of the mighty USA would befall him. The Afghan cocked an antique .303 rifle and aimed it straight at my chest. I now know the meaning of the expression, *"my knees buckled"* as that is exactly what happened. I literally fell over backwards onto the floor of the Kombi. I also saw firsthand the quiet dignity and inner strength of the Afghani people whose personality was so different to all the countries around them, one could understand how they had thrown out every army who had tried to defeat them for hundreds of years. Then in recent times ground down both Russia and the USA into a forced retreat. One could call that nation Stoicstan as the most quietly resilient people I ever met, in a very harsh country.

- Living on a houseboat in Srinagar Kashmir, about which an Indian Emperor wrote, *"if there is a paradise on Earth, it is here, it is here, it is here,"* a sentiment which many, including myself, would agree. I was going for a walk and noticed on a bridge a hundred odd people yelling out and pointing down into the fast, turbulent mountain river. A young child had fallen in and was being washed away yet strangely no one was doing anything. I suddenly realised probably because no one could swim! I jumped in swam down to where the boy was last seen and dived in, but due to the current and the silt, I soon realised he could be well downstream. The visibility was zero, even to discern which way up was a real challenge for me. The little fella was gone, so tragic.

The crowd then broke up and just got on with it, leaving the devastated Mother and me standing on the bank, I was astonished that to the locals a life lost seemed a part of almost daily existence, even in paradise.

- In Malaya after passing over a few of my last resort, *"in the shoe"* US dollars I was hitching a ride on an island freighter to Sumatra. Asleep one rough night somewhere in the Straits of Malacca in a most generous berth under some stairs on the outside metal deck I was suddenly on the move! Sliding right over the side! In a moment I found myself flung up against one of the stanchions supporting the ships railing wires. Had I missed this post and gone between I would have been straight over and into the black deep. In shock I crawled back to my allocated spot shaking and thinking that was a near run thing whilst trying to bind myself in and around the steps with a range of the worst fishing knots ever concocted.

- Travelling through northern Sumatra I had to camp outside villages in the bush which I was well accustomed to by this time. However, I heard what I

168

thought were wild dogs howling like wolves at night which by morning had given me a stiff neck from being jolted upright and nearly swivelling my head 360 degrees all night. In the daylight after packing up I mentioned this to a semi English-speaking local who informed me in a casual way the village dogs were the one's barking. It is their warning there is a *"harimau,"* in the region. Looking quizzically at the gentleman I queried, *"a harrywho?"* He smiled, made a claw like action with his hands and responded. A harimau is a Sumatran tiger roaming the area! I stared at him whilst the enormity of the statement sunk in. My mouth started moving to shape words, but nothing came out. I remember my head dropped, shoulders slumped, and I let out a groan of anguish from the bottom of my soul.

- October, broke and looking for work in Darwin I was told anyone could always get a job picking up sticks following a bulldozer out in the scrub. But no one in the *"top end"* takes on that sort of work in forty degrees plus every day and 99% humidity. My flatmates used to think it was quite humorous of an evening picking me up and saying, *"in the boot please,"* seeing only two eyes and white teeth, the rest of me literally caked in red dirt.

I had been beaten and belted, deceived and abandoned, crossed in love, ripped off and nearly ripped apart, elated, humiliated, wondered and blundered across the world, much of the time alone on a starvation diet and for what?

Little did I know all this adversity I had experienced, would be the best thing that had ever happened to me! The lessons had created a far greater benefit in self-belief, determination and humility. Remembering Oscar Wilde's comment *"Education is a wonderful thing but it is well to remember from time to time that nothing that is worth knowing can be taught."*

I finally made it home to Brisbane three days before Christmas, goal achieved – just! I thought well I had better make some money and I was told times were tough, so I applied for a job remembering being sacked from my first three ventures into the business world I fronted up to the interview by not one but two gentlemen *"suits"*.

Halfway through the interview one of the owners produced a gold Parker pen with a little opal stuck on the top and handing it to me said, *"OK Ray sell me this pen."* I asked how much it was worth and was told $130.00. I quietly placed the pen inside the coat pocket of my brother's suit and asked, *"Gentlemen can we please talk about my wage package?"* The Manager interrupted me saying *"My good man what about the pen?"* I replied, smiling with my best steely look. *"Give me $150.00 and you can have your pen back?"* I was later advised the role had over 100 applicants and surprise, I was hired as an office supplies salesperson. One interview and one job amazing!

After starting I asked my Boss a strange question which just sort of popped out, *"What did I have to do to be the best office supplies salesman in the business?"* and he said, *"My good man, a really good question and I am glad you asked. It is really quite simple just go and get six orders a day, three easy ones in the morning and three in the afternoon."* I enquired from where I would pick up these *"easy"* orders and he said this is your territory right across from where we are at 333 Queen Street, the main street in Brisbane, anything north of here is your *"acre of diamonds,"-* thanks Earl Nightingale. I have never forgotten that very phrase the business must be everywhere I just have to go and pick up the diamonds, meaning make the calls! I walked out the door armed with my blank Quill Order book, head held high in a new suit, crossed the street and into the first hi-rise office building the MMI. Jumped in the first lift to the top floor and started cold calling, by confidently walking into every office.

"NO! No thanks. We have plenty. OUT! Not today or next week. We have dealt with the same company for thirty years. That person is out. We are too busy. Get a real job! Did you not see the sign – no salespeople? Come back, say in a year." Two years later my Boss said to me, *"Congratulations you are the No.2 top carbon paper salesperson in Australia".* Yes, carbon paper, back then it was the cornerstone of our business. This was just prior to photocopiers and carbon paper was a requirement in every office in the land, reams of it were sold and ours was the most expensive on the market! You could scratch it, bash it, bang it on the floor, lick it, stick it, jam it in the door, it was indestructible! I loved my carbon paper and the bonuses it paid too!

I saw other sales representatives come and go in a *"conga line"* in this fine, battling little company, in fact many said there was more turnover of staff than stock! Was this job hard? I still do not know, but I was told what I had to do to be the best, just make six orders a day. Sometimes I would have to make thirty or more calls to come back with my six orders. Other times I was so embarrassed I did not even come back until the following day when I had made my target. I finally worked out this sales business came **down to one thing – keep making the calls by persisting. If you keep making enough calls you will win in the end. Just never stop trying and press on!**

By commitment in sport, I battled my way to play in top Rugby teams and from Third grade at school played in three Grand Finals one A Grade and won a coveted rugby premiership in Second Grade. I coached teams to another two GF's, subsequently captaining an A Grade team, being captain of the Townsville and North Queensland representative teams. I also made the Queensland Country Rugby team and then in 1978 qualified for the Queensland State Rugby squad when the team itself was the strongest provincial rugby side in the world. Won a water polo premiership, collapsed over the line in a marathon and straight into the ambulance tent. Spent five years as a punching bag securing a black belt in Karate, eventually competing and lucking out against a national champion. Won several SLSC Branch titles in a champion beach relay team (mind you the other three were all State and Australian champion athletes so they would always send me off first) beach flags, surf races and yes eventually just like Frank, rowing a surf boat too. I should confess in Holland went to a Disco one night and was amazed at how well the guys could dance unlike my "shuffle jigaboo". So, on the quiet I committed to Arthur Murray's Dance School. Did it pay dividends apart from great fun? I married an exceptionally funny, attractive woman, built on my best friends list and raised two wonderful children. Work wise I went from selling Bic biros for .11c each to some years later selling a property for $105,000,000. I became a Division and State Manager with some great Australian public companies and in the process met some extraordinary talented people, of course all the above was directly underpinned by setting goals and persistence.

What had changed?

I had failed again and again, learned getting up means growth and **quitting gets easier all the time.** I was a completely different person from the other fellow who received the fifteen *"cuts"* in a day. When away I was committed to my original objective to make it back to Oz by Christmas. To achieve this, I had to be single minded and aware, determined and driven, giving this struggle everything, I had and some I never knew I had! I had endured. I had been alone in the world and as a result had unknowingly become someone quite different to what I was before and **indifferent to whatever life could throw my way.** I had responsibility thrust upon me and along with other tasks I then willingly accepted and agreed to pick up the load and just do it. A bit like Robert Frost's classic poem. *"Two roads diverged in a wood, and I - I took the one less travelled by, and that has made all the difference."*

I am not suggesting you should embark on a world journey of self-discovery, something which I fell into like my own abyss. I am saying embrace and commit to the actions in this handbook and life will reward you. My wife and I set a goal for our son and daughter at the start of Year 11. If you graduate to UWA (at the time the highest entry levels of any university in Australia) we will buy you each a car. So, they had a goal and a prize as well and I had given myself a goal of saving the money for the cars, which turned out was just as well! Every year my wife and I would sit down early in January, and each make a list of what we wanted as goals for the year (usually around ten) then discuss and merge our lists together print it off and place on the fridge door. As the year progressed it was genuine fun marking off our achieved goals. Some years we did not do this and guess what happened? Nothing!

Goals are like magnets they pull you towards them. An old rugby friend of mine Ross Crunkhorn, a Major in the Army told me that every nation with a significant army embraces an old German military historian's strategy. Carl Von Clausewitz - The 10 Principles of Warfare (some of which are Manoeuvrability (being able to adapt), Surprise (never give up all your capabilities), Security (when told information in confidence do not share it) and Offensive Action (when you do act do so with total commitment) but **the Number 1 is, you probably guessed it - Selection and maintenance of the Objective or the GOAL. Ross always said when in doubt or lost or confused always refer to Rule Number 1 and you will be OK.**

So, we want to set ourselves up for success. This is what you must do over the next few days. Establish Two **SMART** goals one tangible and one character building. What is a SMART Goal? **SPECIFIC - MEASURABLE – ATTAINABLE - REALISTIC - TIME BASED**

Go through each of those steps and make sure your goal will address each requirement. Please be mindful of this, Viktor Frankl in his wonderful book, *"Man's Search for Meaning"* observed that we all head towards entropy in human nature. Laziness is a natural state, the easy option. If we keep doing what we always have there is a big chance we will get what we always have, but a bit less every time thrown in. **If you aim at nothing you will achieve nothing.** Now draw a horizontal line of where your results are now and aim 20-40% above with some *"kick butt"* goals which attract big effort as little goals attract little focus. Remember if you aim at say an 80% average in your exams you will more than likely end up with 75% as we seem to often fall just short of our aims. In fact, we still achieve so much more than would have been the result with no pre-set goal. So, aim high but a target which is still attainable. **Goals give your life purpose.** They are the greatest achievement creators in the world. Without a clear purpose we wander aimlessly, doing unimportant things, becoming victims of circumstances that befall us and before we know it, we are fully paid-up members of the *"Why me"* club.

Some ideas about your goal?

TANGIBLE GOAL:

What do you want so bad that you do not have and would love to have or achieve? You need to answer this question first, because it is awfully hard to get excited and motivated about achieving something when you do not know what that something is?

- Be the top student in your class. How, get one more point than the current top person.

- In next two years win the highest possible ATAR or Pathway I can by doing one more hour of homework or revision every day.

- Read one book a month every month. Learn chess.

- Set a minimum of a 20 % increase across all subjects for the next year.

- Set a Swimming / Athletic time to achieve. Learn a musical instrument.

- Spend an hour in the library every day after school and Google or read books associated with your subjects.

- Be the best at your chosen activity in the school. Be a trusted popular person in your year by simply giving of yourself, the fine art of building relationships become a Maven (a trusted person who happily passes timely and relevant information onto others – and thus develops lots of contacts and networks with influence).

Approach Mum and Dad and put it to them that if you achieve a certain level, you may be rewarded. In the end it really does not matter what goal you set yourself, I just want you to achieve something challenging, because doing so will then become a habit you will carry with you. So, choose your objective. **And then you must write it down in bold capitals on a piece of paper and display it in your room where you can see it. "If you wake up with a sense of purpose it can save your life if you don't it can destroy it" – Scott Ryan**

CHARACTER GOAL:

This is a goal which is not tangible, you cannot touch it. To have a purpose in life greater than yourself:

- ➤ Mentor a year seven or eight student in your school.
- ➤ Become a person who tries to do *"the right thing"* every time.
- ➤ Pick up any rubbish you see, if you see a toxic environment act, stand up accept the responsibility and volunteer.
- ➤ Never ever complain or criticize anyone or anything.
- ➤ Be on time never be late.
- ➤ Be the person who gets the job done and always finishes.
- ➤ Cook one meal for the family a week.

- Do some volunteer work - this is strong can-do experience.
- Be a friend to everyone you meet and act with humility and be authentic.

As you go along **you may very well find something not quite right,** it could even be some of your friends resent the new you. **But you know adversity means growth.** Identify it and find out what or who may have been holding you back? Then you may have to remove that *"obstacle"*. Then as mentioned **commit the list or statement to somewhere in your room you can see it** every single day or in the pocket of your Blazer. I wore a safety pin for six months on my shirt cuff to remind me of a goal I set. **Fix a term to achieve the goal** – say over a six or twelve-month period. **Then write down ten things you would have to change and or action to achieve the goal.** Then break down into monthly components and measure your performance. **It is even more interesting to note what sort of person do I need to be to realise this objective? We must** always **act with integrity otherwise our objectives are meaningless.**

Note: to go forward you will feel uncomfortable, as you must start doing actions differently than before. However, as you see the goals coming to fruition it is a fine feeling.

By the way, as Bear Grylls said, *"If you are not failing your goals are not big enough, failure is a doorway, if you want to be a winner fail some more. The currency of success is not in muscles and beauty it is in here – in your mind."* I do not want you to worry about what you will be doing in life, only start **making this goal setting a habit as the ideas I am sharing with you are all transferable** and consistent with whatever career you take on:

Journalist / Graphic Designer / Advertising / Hairdresser / Nurse / Doctor /Accountant / IT Code Analyst / Defence Force / Psychologist / Salesperson / Geologist / Fisheries Officer / Ranger / Architect / Engineer / Police Officer / Teacher / Builder / Plumber / Banker / Cyber Security / Jackaroo / Jillaroo .....

It is still OK not to know what you are going to do, in fact until you find something you can be excited about every day, you are still transitioning. *"When the student is ready the teacher will appear"* which means when you see it you will know. Persist with confidence and focus on what you are good at now.

Once you have written down your goals, if you like discuss and share with your parents, mentor and friends. Then every month critically measure your performance. *"If you cannot measure it, you cannot manage it."* **What gets measured gets done!** There will be setbacks, disappointments, frustration but all that means is you are achieving and moving forward, do not take your eyes off the objective. You and it are connected as your mind is already going to work for you. You are on your way. **Do not ever forget,** *"What you vividly imagine, ardently desire, sincerely believe and enthusiastically act upon...must eventually come to pass"*- **Paul Meyer**

Because people with a vision attract the right kind of energy and luck seems to always head their way. If you approach every problem you encounter on that basis then, strange as it may seem, **the force of the universe seems to bend to your will and moves with you.** And as Pareto's Principle predicts 80% of your results will come from 20% of your efforts. Do you know what the 20% is? Selection and maintenance of the objective.

But some take goals to the extreme! I have only met one Billionaire. Spontaneously on shaking hands I quoted him in the newspaper saying, *"Is it true in life, nothing else really matters, life is all about setting goals and achieving them, never starting anything without finishing it and the never-ending stigma of failure?"* He had a laugh as he had said those exact words a few months previously after breaking a 132-year winning streak by another nation and incidentally he offered me a job on the spot!

To help you face the challenges you meet along life's way there is a process many recommend called NLP (Neuro Linguistic Programming - Frogs to Princes by Bandler and Grinder) or mind language resetting which I think is worth considering. I know it works for me and it has been and still is used by top performers in different fields all around the world. It is a bit like creative visualisation where you see the ball going into the netball ring before you throw it, so your mind sets itself up to deliver the outcome. NLP asks you to remember a time when you were the most exhilarated and excited regarding a result you achieved, now recreate or reclaim that feeling in your mind. The elation, the joy, the strength you experienced in the moment. Now take the thought and tie it to an action like clasping your hands together or opening and closing your fist or even just putting your hands on your head in complete focus to recall the feeling. Then visualise the event, let it come into your mind and now take a deep breath and take that power or **anchor point** to the exam or speech or starting blocks as part of the force of your mind now awake within you. My method was to remember the Rugby Premiership we won and the feeling at the clubhouse with the other players that evening when my teammates surrounded me and we all sang our club song. I admired these mates greatly as some of these men, embracing me, were as hard and tough as nails. So purposely our club song went something like this, to the tune of Edith Piaf's Milord. *"We are the Finsbury girls, we wear our hair in curls, we wear our football shorts way up above our knee, when it comes to fights, we run away in fright, we go to ballet classes every Tuesday night la la la la lala."*

If you look at world class athletes just before an event many have little rituals they perform, I can remember a great Australian Rugby goal kicker who used to place the ball down, walk back, stop dead still, look at the goals, the cross bar, the ball, then slowly close and open his left hand the moment before running in to strike the ball (NLP). **You must find a supreme moment to hold onto and use that memory for you to take control.** I used to have to put a particular football sock on the right leg and even on a distinct way before a game, then sit and go deeply inward for a moment until I knew I was ready, sometimes I would even run out onto the field with tears in my eyes.

In business I formed a habit of mentally preparing myself for five minutes before presentations or events by following the above method, without the tears and would feel a surge of confidence and energy **turning pressure into excitement.** Then use the **478** - breathing technique. I learned to have a small mantra to recite being, *"I am calm, I am relaxed, I am in complete control."* You can create your own mantra as it works. Then you will be ready. Because everything is created twice. Your mind first creates the action. If you act like you are excited and relaxed then you allow your mind to go to work to make that thought become real.

Humbly persist in being the person you want to become, and you will see the dream and goal turn into reality. But be warned when it does you may feel like the famous anthropologist Louis Leakey when he finally discovered what he believed was the *"missing link"* between apes and man. He sat down and cried, not in joy because he had finally won after a lifetimes work, but in sadness because his quest was over. **Never forget: The biggest thrill is actually in the doing and the chase to the *"tape."* I CAN GUARANTEE YOU IF YOU WANT TO HAVE MORE FUN AT SCHOOL AND IN LIFE SET YOURSELF A GOAL.**

In case you are curious I made a list of lifetime goals many years ago when I turned twenty - three. Among them were to run a marathon, secure a black belt and win a premiership - but nothing was more important than to *give everything I do everything I have.* Now I only have two remaining lifetime goals. To hang my hat on Poeppels Peg, (the post where the boundaries of QLD, NT and SA all meet) and to learn to play the

Bagpipes! The last one should have been the first one I set many years ago as I learned every day *"do the thing you least want to do first"* and the bagpipes are certainly not the bongos where any tune you play has definite potential! By the way could I ask you to start every day with one action? **Take a moment to tidy your room and put some things away, then read your goal and how you are going to achieve your goal.** In doing that you are setting yourself up for positive actions.

"Once you have the desire, determination and dedication will help you reach your goals. It's very easy to get sidelined or distracted, so it's important to keep focussed on your goals and nothing else. The relentless quest the thing that keeps you going day after day, is your determination. There are no shortcuts in the world or business or sport, there are only goals to be set - and goals to be reached - competition to face and adversity to overcome. Only the truly dedicated persons ever come close to attaining their goals. This is the true test of all great individuals who have the edge - they will not let anything interfere with their goals. That is why so few become champions."- Harvey Mackay

If you sit down today and start setting your goals, you will be on your way. If you wait until tomorrow, you have a 70% chance of going through with the action, if you wait until the weekend, you have just 30% of the goals coming to fruition. If you wait any longer then unfortunately you have wasted your time with this book so read no further, please use it to prop up your desk and in any case the best of luck. **You see people with goals always end up succeeding. What will you do when you do not know what to do?** SET YOURSELF A GOAL! So how do we find the courage to see the goals through? Start building some **character or will or grit**. To learn how to do that you must read on dear reader, read on!

Summary:

- I will set a primary tangible goal to achieve in 6 - 12 months.
- I will also set a secondary goal based on my character development to achieve in 6 - 12 months.
- I will write down ten answers to the question how am I going to achieve my goal? For example, 45 minutes more homework a night, pay strict attention in class, sit at the front of the class, only mix with fellow students who are committed.
- I will remain focussed and disciplined not allowing anything to distract me from my goals. My goals give me a clear purpose and meaning.
- I will write down my goals where I can see them daily and humbly act as if it is impossible for me to fail in my efforts to achieve them.
- I will visualise an achievement I have made and use that moment to give me confidence.
- I will enjoy the journey and not stop until I have achieved my objectives. As I know quitting gets easier all the time

- At all times in pursuit of my goals I will act fairly and do the right thing.

- If you want to have more fun at school and in life set a goal

- I know I will come up short sometimes but that just means I am improving.

- I will ask myself what sort of person I need to become to see these goals happen.

- *"If you wake up with a sense of purpose it can save your life. If you don't it can destroy it".* – Scott Ryan

- I learned this wonderful quote verbatim. You may wish to invoke too? *"I was not delivered unto this world in defeat, nor does failure course in my veins. I am not a sheep waiting to be prodded by my shepherd. I am a lion and I refuse to talk, to walk, to sleep with the sheep. I will hear not those who weep and complain, for their disease is contagious. Let them join the sheep. The slaughterhouse of failure is not my destiny. I will persist until I succeed."* - Og Mandino

- By the way if you want God to have a good laugh-tell God your plans!

- We will not be surprised either when we face those setbacks.
- However, when you commit totally, I mean to go further and harder than ever before a force comes into play some call it Providence or Kismet

ACTION PLAN:

These are my two goals for the following period .... I am totally committed to achieve both goals by this set time nothing must and will stand in my way:

1..

2..

These are some of the actions I am going to change and implement to achieve my goals:

1..

2..

3..

4..

5..

Completion is most important.

CHAPTER 8

CHARACTER AND THE HARD EYE

"Ability may get you to the top but it takes character to keep you there"- **John Wooden**

Past Naples on my trusty Triumph motor bike, doing something stupid again to impress two female hitch hikers I was airborne! Flying in slow motion like a leaping cane toad straight over the handlebars. The bike I now called Trevor was not damaged too much, however the local mechanic shook his head amazed my, *"ticket to adventure"* had even made it this far. The motor had a massive hole in the sump, brakes and gears were completely worn out and in his own words which he somehow found so funny, my trusty Triumph was a *"limoni amico"* or as we would say these days *"a real lemon friend."* Apart from the acute embarrassment, I was lucky not to break my neck. I could take some solace that my unbroken reputation of being ripped off in every port was still intact! Plus, thanks to Pepe the mechanic I was now bike less, but twenty pounds richer! I spent a few days in the local forest, under my tarpaulin, considering my options. Then I was off again, this time I was hitch hiking too.

Yes, life is difficult. At my old school it was surprising how many fine students repeated their final year and then applied themselves totally to their studies. These students had committed the previous year to rowing or football, hence were too preoccupied and unable to deliver the required effort in the classroom. Or their marks were simply not high enough. So, they repeated a year, channelled all their energy into their studies and made their goal – another year so what! In the great scheme of your life an extra year here or there really means nothing. Plus, there are plenty of bridging courses *"out there."* if you wish to deeply commit again after school. Or when you leave school and if you are not going onto a Trade or University or do not have a job lined up the concept of your own *"gap year"* travelling is worth considering.

In the first term of Year 12 contact your local council and attend the next job expo. The more opportunities you can expose yourself to the better off your decision-making process will be for a career. Familiarise yourself with skillsroad.com.au and jobjumpstart.gov.au. Also volunteer work opens doors.

After school days are over whatever you do, do not make the mistake of doing nothing! That would be a grave error because you just get older and weaker inviting in anxiety and depression. I started sleeping in longer doing less exercise, hitting the fridge hourly and crowing like the secretary of the Whingers Society! Join a club or volunteer as before you know it, the year will be gone and you may wind up becoming the last of these three types of people: those who make it happen, those who watch it happen and those who say - what happened? If you still wonder what you should do, the best self-improvement coach ever (Dale Carnegie) said, *"I must lose myself in action lest I wither in despair."* So just get active and mobile. **How, set yourself a goal and follow the road map!** Do not let your mind play the blame game saying, *"woe is me."* You already know life is tough and you will already have encountered a few land mines, but now you are becoming focussed and determined a bit like, well, a young Paladin. Hit the reset button, become a little bit obsessive but with a smile and say yes, I get **IT** from NOW on I promise myself I will do the best I can!

Allow me to reinforce to you the two hardest things in the world - **Getting started and never quitting.** I had learned by some sort of quiet transitioning on my world trip some key facts:

- I discovered I used to open my mouth before thinking and through circumstances learned to be the one who just shut up and listened
- I learned to be always focussed on the objective despite being confronted with obstacles like foraging wild animals
- I learned to try hard to be better prepared than others which means always being aware and after consideration and listening to others finally asking questions
- Making sure I never shirk any task. When things go wrong have a good laugh
- I learned to keep going forward step by step, as Charles Dickens said. *"Those who learn endurance are they who call the whole world brother."*

After returning from overseas, when I was playing Senior Rugby in the Reserve Grade (the Second Team) we embarked on a course to win the Grand Final. As the season progressed our team developed a habit of starting training even before the A Grade team and finishing after everyone else was back showering in the clubhouse. Due to our captain Mike Thies, we had a most disciplined approach and through following his example no one ever cut any corners in 400 metre runs or miscounted fifty push ups. His mantra on the field was short and repetitive, *"get your heads up!"* Hard to become discouraged with your head up and people like that exude an aura called *"presence"*. Regarding tactics Mike in his position at first five was our key player. However, on the odd occasion an opposition team member would attempt to, shall we say physically disrupt the execution of his winning strategy by sticking him with an elbow to the jaw or late tackle. He had a secret deployment for this too. One of our own team members was chosen and instructed to call the other player to account by whatever means necessary! The instruction was quite succinct with two words only, *"get him."* Only years later we understood the one selected for this (guess who) task if he was ever penalised by a *"send-off"* was considered expendable and deemed collateral damage! Rule Number One in action.

On the odd occasion I would be promoted to the A Grade I was surprised by the talking amongst the players in the team, whereas in the Reserve Grade only two people could speak - the halfback and our captain, such was the discipline. **The best leaders are always disciplined.** As the season progressed, I asked some of my teammates if they did any extra training (apart from our Tuesday and Thursday sessions and the game on Sundays) as I felt compelled to do with 10k runs, weights and together with my brother driving our parents mad punching a heavy bag which hung from the rafters under the house. Every person I spoke to in the team was doing something extra and had never told a soul. There was something special happening here! **No one wanted to be the weak link and were committed to the team and the goal.**

I never thought too far in front and the Finals soon came upon us. I was told we had won twenty-one games straight! I had no idea we were so successful, as such was the determination to give everything we had in every game we played. We then lost the first semi-final between the top two teams which was a real shock, then we came back and won the Preliminary Final and then smashed our opponents in the Grand Final by 34-6. I still find it hard to explain what happened there. Suffice to say the character shown by every player throughout the season galvanised us into a team who, on that last and most important Sunday, we would not quit and would not be beaten. I can still remember during our last few weeks of training coming home so exhausted and physically drained that I struggled to eat my dinner and had to drag myself out of bed the next morning to go and sell my beloved carbon paper. The point is we were not the super men in the club in First Grade where some also played for the State and for the country as Wallabies!

But we devoured something in large doses: discipline and resilience.

So strong were these attributes we were able to deliver such consistent pressure on the opposition, they eventually just caved in. **We had by this extra effort**

each tapped into a strength we never knew we had and it responded. I believe it was the force of our will and our focussed group intent we placed on every team made them eventually crack under the pressure. Throughout the season we had been tested like never before to the point of total exhaustion and failure, again and again without any of us saying a word, well a few! **The failures led to more focus, more determination and giving it all we had.** We plunged into depths where we used to joke, *"The pain we generated was sheer bliss."* **Also, the determination was somehow contagious and spread into other areas of my life** with good events and friendships coming to the fore, making me someone who I felt perhaps even this ex-loser could be depended upon. This value of not quitting has never failed me. I had learned if one keeps going eventually the rock will crack.

Underpinning all of this was character. We created character from our own discipline before our skills were honed. We developed character from the pain we endured and the goal we had set. So, remember, **character always comes before capability.**

This is a lesson about individual grit and resilience but there is another important lesson here too. **When a group of people jointly commit to a common objective and together strive to achieve the target your chances of success multiply.** You do not need the same goal you just all need to have a collective will to reach your aim. One of you may want an A in Science, the other an increase of 15% across all subjects, but you both strive for the objective. Working in unison therein lies real power. Two, three of more can run together towards set goals with much greater success than if you all ran individually. As the old proverb rightly tells: *"In unity there is strength."*

I mentioned before you may end up saying *"enough is enough I did not sign on for this"* and just call it quits. You could call that *"drowning in the shallow end,"* since all you really must do is just stand up and say to yourself with a smile. ***"Hold on I am not done yet."*** Now this is important, when training to run the marathon, so many times I just wanted to pack it in and walk but I started setting small goals by saying to myself if I can see the next hill, *"I can make it."* Then look ahead again, pick out another object and set that as my goal. I am convinced at the very moment when your whole being is screaming to stop what you are doing in mind and or body and you **press on** for another one or five or ten minutes is when a strange, almost spiritual growth happens physically and mentally, giving you an edge and spurring you on to a rare place which will make all the difference. **It is at these times the muscle of courage grows stronger.**

Now I hope I can say you are committed to your task 100 per cent, not just 90 per cent but with the dogged, fighting, determined extra 10% you will discover that, when you dig deep within, you uncover the golden seam wherein lies your success. Of course, you will stumble and fall, but when you do, as you now know that is when you will find the treasure.

"Courage does not always roar. Sometimes courage is the quiet voice at the end of the day saying, 'I will try again tomorrow." Mary Anne Rademacher

There was another factor at play in the above stories and it is one I have noticed in every success I have experienced throughout life – discipline. In every sporting action, whether playing or coaching and most importantly in career roles I enjoyed, the most fruitful and the most fun was when the strongest discipline was a component. I learned discipline brings out the best in you and others and helps form the best winning relationships. When coaching a start-up Under 14 and Under 15 football team I set some rules as follows; we start training when the last person arrives, we train for one hour, no swearing, no spitting, no running others down for making a mistake and we set our goal to be the fittest team in the competition and to win the Grand Final. With a team of boys some who had never played rugby before, over two years we won every game apart from three. Unfortunately, two of these were the last game each year, the Grand Finals! Life sure is challenging!

It was wonderful to hear from a few of the parents of the boys who wrote to me confidentially saying their sons thrived on the sense of meaning, purpose, and discipline we were building.

So do not shirk, but rather welcome the hard taskmaster, all that rigidity is good for you and builds character. I was on beach patrol at our surf club, ours was a quiet location and I was sucking my thumb wondering why I had chosen to chase a crab shoulder deep down a hole when I noticed someone waving to me beyond the break. I was just about to wave back when I realised, I had my first ever rescue on my hands! Donning the Torpedo buoy, I was off at *soft sand speed*. On reaching the hapless person after suffering a few bangs on the head and kicks I managed to connect the flotation buoy and dragged him back to the shore. Totally spent I unclipped the bloke who was OK and bent over hands on my knees shaking with exertion. I thought I could have just saved a life! After a moment I stood up only to find the gentlemen casually walking up to the car park. What did I expect? I only knew I had a lot more growing up to do.

Sometimes you may even want to jokingly yell at the universe, *"Is that the best you got?"* Then just in case - better say, *"Only kidding!"* Tell you why later.

Now we need you to build into yourself some more armour and what people call a *"hard eye."* Do you know what a hard eye is? I am sure you may have seen it at some time, perhaps from your own Dad......I sure did! Or if you are ever in a Court room and are required to give evidence before the Magistrate who lords over his domain, elevated behind the massive mahogany desk embossed with the coat of arms. The one who can turn you to stone with one look as you start stuttering, knowing in a heartbeat, he can see right through you. Or the implacable stare of someone who does not bluff and will stand up no matter what confronts them. Do not worry if you have not seen it yet. You will see these people as you grow. Watch the eyes of some great achievers and you will see it. Steely will like you have never known before and unblinking determination. The interesting thing is many do this unconsciously, but their personality is such you can read it through their eyes alone.

I had a role for a few years amalgamating redevelopment sites which comprised acquiring older properties on high density land zonings suitable for new hi-rise apartments. I heard there was a serious developer in town from Melbourne trying to source this type of product and I was fortunate to receive a call for an appointment. Fortune was smiling having just completed a successful acquisition resulting in a fifteen-storey luxury apartment building being constructed on the land I had consolidated so I was now selling sixty-five luxury apartments as well! I was competent and confidently looking forward to meeting this *"big hitter."* In due course he was shown to my office with his Personal Assistant - a man of about sixty! I invited the gentlemen to sit down, had about sixty seconds of courtesy chat by his PA, then I was struck, transfixed by the most penetrating eyes I had ever seen. The main man asked me three or four really searching questions I think to test my knowledge. Then silence. Someone had to say something, so off I gushed, twenty-five minutes later it was over, and they were gone. I had a cold sweat and felt physically exhausted, never in my life had I been interrogated with such gentle and yet intensive persuasion. His eyes seemed unblinking, never moving from me. This *"kingpin"* had dragged every ounce of knowledge out of me, as I burst forth trying with the very fibre of my inflated ego to impress him. He had what I learned was the *"hard eye."* The look of the seasoned campaigner in business or life trained to the peak of savage efficiency with of course always an objective.

You will know when you meet someone like the Melbourne gentlemen, and I started to learn that when you are talking you are learning nothing. The skill as mentioned in Chapter One is keeping your mouth shut and to get the other party talking whilst you remain focussed. Therein the power lies. In fact, to be a good listener is an exceptionally fine art and requires you to really concentrate.

The hard eye person looks right at you, not in an aggressive way but in a way, you know will not stand for any nonsense or *"puffery."* The intensity of their character is such they are mostly people with values and integrity. If one adds empathy to that mix, with that combination it is not hard to see why women nowadays are becoming so prominent in business.

And believe me the *"hard eye"* is not an exclusively a male thing. Women are nowadays becoming the dominant force in many fields of commerce and industry. In my field, the property industry, according to realestate.com in Australia in 2018 female sales brokers averaged 65% of the workforce. Could it be because they do not have the same ego driven mindset as males? In hindsight I think a woman would have facilitated the previous interview to a more productive relationship and outcome. As in case if you are not aware already, females are much better listeners than the males. They understand life is not all about proving their status. This gives them a distinct advantage in negotiation and building relationships.

I mentioned previously who is the one person in the world you could speak most fluently about? YOU ARE of course. Engage the other person to talk about themselves. This is important - develop the fine art of becoming an active listener. People of character are honest so be genuine. So many times, over the years I listen and let people talk then encourage them to say more about their lives and I learn so much and they walk away with respect and gratitude for you and all you did was – be nice, be quiet and be honest. Be aware of the person who applies this to you, they are in control and powerful. When it is being done to me, I really enjoy it because I can try to humbly *spruik* about how good I think I am but I also know I am dealing with someone with substance.

Of course, there will be a price to pay to earn your skill in being quiet but at the same time very *"present."* This may be sometimes when you would otherwise be *"gainfully"* improving another type of your armour, playing computer games or peering into the open fridge or thinking about how to avoid doing what you know you should be doing.

A good friend, Steve Missen was a champion boxer. He told me just before the bell when they would meet in the ring, he made sure he never blinked and focussed eye to eye. If his opponent looks at him and swallows, he knew he had him. This is a truism. **So, when you meet anyone, look them in the eye and show them you are genuine in everything you say and do and whatever you do - do not swallow!**

Also try to always sit and walk with your eyes straight ahead. That is your head up. Raise it about 30cm so you are looking parallel to the ground and notice as others too notice your view of the world change. Building character takes a lifetime so take it slowly and meaningfully.

Summary:

- I will start building some real determination into everything I do even when I want to stop. "Those who learn endurance are they who call the whole world brother."
- I will persist a bit more and then just a bit more.
- Whenever I meet anyone, I will look them right in the eye and be a genuine person.

- I know to build my character I must have a purpose, be honest and feel for others.
- Never will I *"drown in the shallow end"* I will stand up and go on.
- I love and thrive on discipline – it is good for me.
- Everything I will ever want, or need is outside my comfort zone. So I get used to being uncomfortable. Walk with that head up!
- I accept when situations go wrong for me many will not be there, and I will not be surprised.
- I know I will fail but I will accept I have done my best and go again.

ACTION PLAN:

1. How am I going to develop my determination and grit?

   ....
   ....

2. I will practice looking people in the eye and being genuine.

   ....
   ....

3. I will remain committed to my objectives which are?

   ....
   ....

CHAPTER 9

STOIC RESILIENCE

"You will fail by adversity or be forged by adversity."

Walking down the street from Howrah railway station in Kolkata (Calcutta), I thought I had seen it all, but it was not the case. Blind children begging and deformities like amputation of legs had been inflicted on kids as babies. As otherwise they would not, could not survive. People literally living in cardboard boxes and rag pickers competing with the monstrous vultures on the massive, steaming rubbish tips in this city, like no other on Earth. On the street a totally naked starving woman in the gutter grabbed me by the ankle and would not let go crying *"baksheesh."* As I tried to pull away a policeman came to my *"rescue"* and with a baton started belting this poor lady into submission. I walked away. The thought of what happened to that woman still lives with me. I think that moment was about the final piece in the jigsaw of the total breaking down of my own self-importance resiled to accept how heartless the world can be.

"Do not worry it is just a stage you are going through." If I heard that statement from my parents one more time my school bag was leaving home at warp speed to a galaxy far, far away. Angry, careless, irritable, determined and fed up with a bad attitude and all emotions firing simultaneously – hold on I must be a teenager!

A good mate of mine, like all of us has had many tough times and his sense of humour always inspires me. When he had a recent setback, I asked him how he was feeling? His response, *"It's lonely in the saddle when your horse is dead."* Please do not ask what that means! **In my experience you cannot beat someone who laughs in the face of adversity.** One of the players in William Shakespeare's King Lear made the following wonderful statement, ***"Make content thy fortunes fit, tho' it raineth and raineth every day."*** So, the purpose of this chapter is to discuss how you might go about developing the capacity to be steadfast in yourself. **Pain is always coming into our lives. It is there to help us grow and when we personally *"sook out"* or whinge or ask, *"why is life so cruel?"* We are remaining childlike and as a person our capacity to accept and endure is falling. So, what should we do?**

Well, there is another especially important life skill or character trait to help see you through life's many challenges. **I want you to embrace a form of managing your life called Stoicism.** Stoicism was refined and flourished at the time of the Roman Empire due to a Greek philosopher called Epictetus. A man whose ideas have since been followed by some of the greatest leaders in history.

A stoic person remains unmoved by outside influences and outcomes. Where they encounter a problem, they do whatever they can to remedy the situation and what they cannot fix - they simply accept. Definition: a person who can endure pain or hardship without showing their feelings or complaining.

A stoic person can:

- Be embarrassed and laugh about it.

- Try and fail miserably, accept the outcome, and try again.

- Be left out of a group or team and smile, wish the others the absolute best and mean it.

- Be alone and still joyful.

- Be still, alone in a group and be comfortable.

- Rejected and fallen out of love and somehow keep smiling knowing you will be OK.

- Recognise you are different because you are becoming indifferent and more accepting to the challenges life throws at us. *"To a stoic the obstacle is the way"- Ryan Holliday.*

- That is a stoic – and thinking like a stoic is a powerful way to think!

If I can do something I will, if I cannot so be it, I will choose my own state of mind about any matter. *"The problem is always how we choose to see the problem"* *– Stephen Covey.* **Our perception of the matter or how we see it makes the problem manifest itself in us. So what story are we going to tell ourselves**

when visited by an unforeseen circumstance? That is purely our choice.

Marcus Aurelius the great Roman Emperor and scholar of Epictetus said, *"Look well into yourself for there is a source of strength that will always spring up if you will always look and look not for any greater harm than this – destroying the trustworthy, self-respecting, well-behaved person within you - **only you can destroy you.**"* – What a fine statement!

Your mind must be stronger than your feelings. **This is a critical skill to learn and live. EVERY POOR DECISION YOU MAKE WILL ALWAYS COME FROM EMOTION RATHER THAN YOUR MIND.** In particular as a teenager! You cannot control some outcomes and certainly not the thoughts of others, but you can certainly control how you are going to think and then act. I can recall so many bad decisions, all were based on my feelings not my mind. How you choose to think about situations will determine how you respond. You are unmoved by circumstances, but you can still be concerned and act when you know it is proper to do so and give it your all. Living like this takes courage. The

Greek Aristotle (350 BC) one of the greatest philosophers who ever lived said, *"Courage is the mother of all virtues without it you cannot effectively perform everything else."*

Whilst employed as the State Real Estate Manager, one of our best rural sales staff had sold a massive pastoral property to a major client on a *"take it as it is"* basis which meant it included all the plant and equipment (bulldozers, trucks, housing, machinery, vehicles, and thousands of prime cattle). After payment it turned out one of the vehicles was faulty and the new owners requested it be replaced. Value probably about $20k. I discussed this with the salesperson, and it became apparent unless we compensated the buyers in some way, they had indicated they would revisit (code for seek competitors offers) all their business streams with us. This included insurance, merchandise, livestock, real estate and finance. All up, this amounted to a massive annual contribution in revenue to our firm. A decision meant a short trip, which many staff found extremely long as it required a visit to the State Manager. So, with much trepidation up I went up in the lift to the big office on the security floor to have the variation agreed to by the man where the *"buck stops."* The matter was to be determined by the State Manager as on the balance of probabilities for such a major client it seemed, *"a given"* to only negotiate a deal with some sort of compensation for these most valuable clients. Peter Maxwell asked, *"Did they acquire the property "as is" and understood in the agreement they had to do all their own diligence and signed the contract accordingly?"* I answered, *"Yes sir!"* He quietly said to me, ***"We must always hold the line and honour our agreements otherwise we may be seen to be less than what we are."*** He quietly and stoically said, *"No."* I was shocked! In doing so I was convinced we risked losing the entire account to do the right thing on a value or principle. As it turned out the client stayed with us now with absolute respect and gave us even more business than before. Our Boss a stoic man of character.

A stoic refuses to be offended or influenced by any one thing or any circumstances. When confronted with a moral crisis they remain true to their value system. There are no shades of truth you do the right thing or you do not.

Life is hard. We know that. But once we accept that life is hard, we start to understand that **our greatest growth always seems to come from our darkest times**.

This interesting aspect of believing and developing the mental toughness of the stoic is that once you start making some challenging decisions, change starts to emerge and compliment you in several aspects of your life. If you start training in the gym strangely your commitment to other tasks increases as you develop this habit of intestinal fortitude! **You see once you decide not to be phased by challenges and negative outcomes, unknowingly your own willpower is coming into play without you even being aware.** The actual challenge makes you better than if you had never faced the adversity at all. Studies show that students who exercise a higher level of willpower in their life perform better over the year than students with higher IQ's whose performance remains consistent. **Those who *"see off"* challenges have fewer absences, play less pretend computer games and in the end are more likely to achieve higher outcomes.**

To understand what I am trying to say can you make yourself angry now! It is impossible. Anger is a response to a stimulus or a provocation. Your mind decides to fire up and become angry. So, if you find yourself feeling annoyed, angry or irritable it is you who has the problem.

The Roman philosopher Seneca said whenever you feel the onset of anger the best way to contain it is to be quite still and do nothing: don't walk or move or say anything. If you allow your body to do whatever it wants the anger inside you will simply increase.

Generally, there will be one of three reasons for our anger:

1. You are hungry so your energy / tolerance levels are low

2. You are tired which will make you irritable

3. Someone or something has hurt you and you are resentful

No thanks I choose not to panic! **The greatest remedy for fear and anger is DELAY.** Have the courage to re set and take back control of you and your emotions. **Stoics do not judge or react they observe.** Do you think you could become a stoic for life? This would be one of the best actions you could ever embrace. My older brother was a stoic long before me. He is a risk taker in business and has been most successful. He seizes opportunities, wins and loses but the key in the *"game"* as he calls it is simply to keep trying and thereby to learn and over time you start to win more often than you lose. One time he quoted anthropologist and author Ralph Blum to me. *"Everything we experience has a beginning a middle and an end, so walk not back from the passage into darkness, when in deep water become a diver"*. It took me a while to find the diamond in this statement but we both know it now, don't we? When things are difficult or we are challenged, or when we are facing a wellspring of conflicting emotions at the prospect of the constant changes' life brings, struggling only makes things worse. Trying to claw your way to the surface or leap out of a hole usually is not a possibility. Knowing when to allow things to change (and to embrace endings) is part of life! **So sometimes you must become the diver and fully embrace whatever is happening and adapt**

with one provision, your own moral code is not jeopardised.

There are wonderful things to discover going into the unknown which need not represent *"failure"* and catastrophic loss ... after all, challenge is our avenue to a new and better way of being and growth. There is no *"ending"* or change without some kind of re-birth! The winter must end for there to be roses blooming in the spring. The same as the amazing change in a cumbersome caterpillar to be re born a butterfly. So, no matter what circumstance befalls you personally, first find a way to say to yourself; **I am not emotionally moved, I am indifferent to that event. In fact, I willingly accept the problem because it is mine and I must play the hand I am dealt to resolve or live with it and I will acknowledge it as my pain alone to bear and wear it with a smile. Because I am a stoic and unmoved and I have accepted the situation. I know because peace is found in acceptance. This is a real person with character and this one attitude can change your life.**

When another good friend of mine had a setback and was ruminating on the event when asked how he felt he would always respond. *"Well last time I felt like this my rocking horse had died."* This retort always elicited a laugh from me, admiration for his stoicism and his jibe about being a child. This willing acceptance of the event is being a stoic. The great American baseball player Babe Ruth held a world record in hitting the most home runs in a career that stood for decades. Not many know he also struck out more times than any other player in history. He just kept stepping up and swinging that bat with everything he had......... that is the approach of a stoic.

The King was not happy, his Court Jester had made one politically incorrect joke too many, so he hauled him up before the nobles and Paladins at court and in front of them all said to him: "I have had enough Jester. You will be flogged, speared, hung up and drawn and quartered tomorrow at dawn." The Jester pleaded for more time and in desperation said, "Sire if you give me one year - I will teach your horse how to talk!" Everyone burst out laughing at his final joke, but he promised the King he was serious. The King then said, "OK you really are a great clown I will give you one year from this day." All the friends of the Jester gathered around saying you must be mad, that is impossible, and the Jester stoically replied, "You may very well be right, however in one year, the King may be dead, I may be dead or the horse might talk."

The moral of this story is simply this: anything can happen given time.

You see we never see life coming. If you just remain stoic and resilient, you will be amazed at how often events can change in your favour. In my life when confronted with dire situations I always just did whatever I could to remedy the issue and once I was sure I could do no more, I stopped worrying. Instead, I just pressed on and looking back somehow over and over, something would eventuate providing the solution to the matter or an alternative path, a way around the problem somehow appeared, whereas if I had given up who knows?

I am convinced if you do everything you can every time that will be enough.

It seems as if some force of nature comes to assist those who persist. When a grit of sand finds its way into an oyster and proceeds to irritate the muscle which makes the oyster sick, it covers the grit with enamel to ease the pain and a wondrous thing happens - a pearl is created. Therefore, as the old saying goes: *"It takes a sick oyster to make a pearl thank God for suffering it ennobles you."* **Own your own problems, confront and accept them and smile with stoic indifference, because you understand they are yours alone, given to you to make you stronger. All you must do is endure and try to laugh**.

Ajahn Brahm the popular Buddhist teacher, believes that a clever and effective way of helping us to overcome and accept any problem that comes our way is to first listen with respect to the problem then say, *"very good."* Whenever you encounter some obstacle or trouble, just say to yourself, *"very good."* I know this may sounds a bit *"wacky"* but in every obstacle, no matter how dire, there is some good to be mined, some lesson of value to be learned. Try it next time you may feel disappointed or discouraged by something. Just say aloud – *"very good."* At the very least you will have a laugh and those around you will be intrigued. In every challenge life throws at you there is a message trying to be delivered to you, to give you strength. You just must realise it. So, no matter what, the outcome may be, *"very good"!* Indeed, **our attitude creates OUR reality**.

Of course, a problem shared is also a problem half solved. So, I recommend when you encounter an apparently intractable problem you do not keep it entirely to yourself. Seek the counsel of your good friend or parents or mentor because two heads are better than one. But it is still your problem and all you will do in talking to others about it is flesh out the answer you more than likely knew in the first place. **So, accept it and resolve it if you can, and if not just press on.** You will look back six months later and say, *"Gee that was rough, but I came through it"* and the muscle of resilience grows stronger.

A few times over the years I met a person for the first time who really impressed me with being successful and a genuinely nice person, so I would ask them what line of business they were in and often it would be Insurance. Once I was liaising with an older associate called Bill. I discovered that he had once been an insurance salesperson for a leading company and I asked him to tell me what the job was really like. Selling insurance involved endless hard gut wrenching knocking on doors or opening the telephone book and start making calls. He smiled and responded, *"My friend for most of my life I was a rock breaker."* He paused then for a moment with a curious smile. As I stared at him in amazement, unsure of what he meant, he continued. *"Yes, I used to break rocks. You see I would start with a huge boulder and a sledgehammer and I would keep swinging the sledgehammer until the rock broke in half, then I would pick up a smaller Lump hammer and smash away at the halves until they broke into quarters and then eighths and then sixteenths. Then I grab an even lighter hammer and keep hammering away until all I have is tiny little rocks and with a tiny little jeweller's hammer I would break these pieces into sand, which dropped at my feet. Then I would just kick it away and go and pick up the big hammer again and find another boulder."* It is such a great analogy for life and success in life - **slow and steady, remorseless and stoic will win every time.** I have never forgotten that story and I hope you do not either **– to find happiness and be successful we must become Rock Breakers.**

There was an elderly man I knew called Jonas Pampel, who was from my father's generation. Jonas used to push himself at gym workouts so hard he would sweat profusely and be literally soaked. I would worry he was over doing his physical capacity as he was well into his sixties. We became acquaintances, he was different from Australians he had some sort of, *"Je ne sais quoi,"* which was particularly European along with a wonderful generosity of spirit. Indeed, he was one of the most humble, authentic human beings I have ever met. The other peculiar thing is Jonas never stopped smiling and his eyes were so deep they used to jolt me when he looked my way. Jonas owned an ice cream shop. One day after a workout we were chatting and I noticed a mark on his arm, which was well, odd. I asked him what it was, thinking he may have been an ex-sailor, as he was a tough man, and the tattoo may have had a nautical story about going *"round Cape Horn"* or similar. However, as I looked closer, I noticed it was in fact an old number on his forearm and as it dawned on me, he responded simultaneously, *"My Auschwitz number."* (In World War Two Auschwitz was an infamous Nazi Death Camp). As he spoke those chilling words he did the strangest thing - he smiled at me. I could have fallen over.

Immediately it all fell into place, here was a man who had been to hell, suffered unimaginably in the death camps of WW 2, where six million innocent men, women and children were murdered. He told me a story where every day as the prisoners filed out to work, a German SS Officer would stand in front of the queue, assess each person and with a flick of his finger to the left or right, determine who would go to work and who would go to die in the gas chambers. Jonas was one of a few who survived and he showed an outlook all was well with the world and yet trained like his life depended on it. To say he radiated an aura would not be inappropriate. What was the feeling he gave to me? I felt like I just wanted to embrace him, and my heart broke with love for this so resilient, gentle soul. **To me Jonas was a stoic and a person with true grit. There was nothing he could do about his past circumstances then or now. He could not change his past so why be miserable about it? He chose not only to be indifferent, but he chose also to be happy.**

You see mostly the ones who appear to become most satisfied in life and high achievers as well, are not the ones who became Duxes of the schools or the champion athletes. They have the IQ to matriculate and exceed at university and sports careers, leading to highly fruitful vocations. But many find themselves somewhat bound by the strict pathways imposed by precedents. Another example in the SAS Who Dares Wins TV programme, one of the veteran instructor's stated, *"The young muscled up recruit with all the tattoos never makes the final cut."*

The ones who run in the places down the rungs at school who may not be blessed with outstanding brilliance or talent on the field, often become the happiest. These are the resilient triers with no limits, **who just give a little bit more every time than they did the time before, who refuse to give up and remain quietly stoic.** Those who accept the vagaries of life, it's hurt and damages, its unfairness and even cruelty and still say to themselves, like Jonas did: **I can handle this, I can endure and THIS TOO SHALL PASS.** But also, do not forget so will the good times! So, stoicism is all about choosing - to choose one's attitude in any given set of circumstances, to choose one's own way. But what if you have lost your way and do not know what to choose? Now again I ask you this fundamental question, *"What will you do when you do not know what to do?"*

I used to have a boss who, whenever there was a major problem, would disappear on a country trip for a few days. I would be concerned he was *deserting the ship*, but seven times out of ten when he returned the matter would be resolved, if not he would then address the problem. The lesson being whenever confronted it is often best to simply do nothing, do not react, take it on board, say *"very good"* and remain indifferent. Then give it a couple of days and re visit if the concern is still apparent.

When in doubt – *"do nothing"* or *"when in doubt turnabout"* are great maxims. When you do not know what to do or cannot find a solution simply do nothing and wait and watch. This attitude will solve so many stresses for you in life, as so much in our lives just seems to work itself out. Of course, sometimes we do not have the privilege of time on our side – that is a moment of truth. You have to then act with your mind, ask yourself, what is the right thing to do here?

"Define the moment or the moment will define you."
Walt Whitman. Then act decisively.

I met a bloke one day who wanted to train with us, and he turned up at the appointed time already covered in sweat. I said, *"Mate you look like you have already had a decent workout"* and he said in a very calm English accent (sorry Welsh, he discreetly pointed out to me). *"Well, I have just been for a run to that big rock down the road and back."* I nearly fell over as the only big rock for kilometres, painfully, I knew was a gut busting three-hour jog away and back. I asked him what he did for a living, and he set on me with a hard eye, stood upright and stated in a way I will never forget, *"I'm a soldier."* His name was Alan Bennett he was a Sergeant with the Welsh Guards on a special charitable leave in Australia after coming back from the Falklands War. No wonder he could jog so far, in the Falklands, in one instance his mates Chinook helicopters were literally *"blown up"* and the platoon had to *"yomp"* (your ordinary marching pace) 90 kilometres (two marathons) with 40 kilos of ammunition and ordinance on their back in two days, then fight someone, if necessary to the death.

Alan told me a story where he had in his platoon a few supporting Gurkhas who are recognised as amongst the most feared soldiers on the planet and how they would attack an enemy held position. Being on a strict timeline to attend to the Falklands matter and the enemy *"contacts,"* his stories left me in awe and speechless - which I am told is sometimes quite hard to do! Alan said on occasions when the Argentinians were proving difficult to dislodge from a position and to avoid indiscriminate casualties by artillery, his Commander would bring out a loud hailer and over the speaker in Spanish advise, *"If you do not surrender right now, we will be forced to send in the Gurkhas."* Alan said we usually did not have to wait long before the *"Argies"* would come out with their hands up!

The Gurkhas are stoics personified, **whose reputation is built on their ability to quietly accept and take on any mission to completion**. I knew then Britain had sent their finest down there with Alan and remarkably he was cheerful, unperturbed and such a professional in fact it was quietly unnerving - he was indeed a soldier. Before he returned home, he gave me one of his Sergeants flak jackets which I still have and cherish. **Another example of a stoic who accepted this deadly deployment with the right attitude and delivered and moved on with life.**

So, we all are under pressure sometimes and consistent pressure turns into stress and stress will debilitate you. **But if you are indifferent to pressure, you can throw it off and remain emotionally in charge of yourself.** When you are in control you are a powerful unit - **life is a lot about emotional control.** As mentioned previously, scientists have recently learned the receptors in our brains causing stress and excitement are **the same neurotransmitters! So - will I be stressed, or will I choose to be excited by this experience?**

Another very good quick fix for anxiety is to splash your face with cold water. Called the *"diving reflex"* the action immediately reduces heart rate and induces better control.

As Winston Churchill said, *"I like a man who smiles when he fights."* He meant, of course, that he liked a man (or woman) who does not run from fear but who instead is excited and engaged by it and who, in doing so, exudes and manifests courage by looking into the face

235

of adversity and challenging it head on. Smiling during the contest is one way to not only embolden oneself but also to disarm and discourage the opponent, whether that opponent is an actual person or a condition. The person may not know the outcome, but they are coming in with the right mindset and I do not know about you but someone who is smiling and relaxed as they came at me in a confrontation always made me nervous. Has this type of person elected to be stressed or excited by their situation? For example, watch a video of Kathy Freeman in her 400-metre win at the Sydney Olympics or the boxer Muhammed Ali both always totally focussed mentally, totally in control and seemingly relaxed.

Mark Twain once said, *"I am an old man and I have known a great many troubles - most of which never happened"* You know you will be confronted over and over, become anxious and if you allow it, even become depressed but do not forget a great proportion of these worries simply will not even eventuate. You see, *"Worry is paying interest on trouble before it even happens."*- William Inge **Therefore, if you can do something to resolve a worry do it and if you cannot accept it with a smile.**

Women on average live longer than males and there is mounting evidence one of the main reasons is because they do not take silly risks. Studies are suggesting women can also handle pain better and longer and are more likely to survive in challenging circumstances. Plus, there is an old saying, *"The female is deadlier than the male."* Studies are showing in armies around the world the woman is proving to be a more efficient, deadlier soldier when it comes to the crunch and can emotionally move forward sooner in recovery. They are in fact in a crisis more stoic and resilient and a more bankable commodity. Why is this so? Is it because nature chose the female to carry and continue all life, so they had to be tougher? My point being in many instances your best support when you need it could very well be that quiet one rather than the school shot putt champion! Also taking the time to take three deep slow breaths or 478 breathing will help every time before any challenge. Now this is so important: **If you overthink any matter, you will become anxious. So do not believe everything you think. You will find in most cases your anxiety is caused by you overthinking. When you are at peace with the past in acceptance and accepting of** the future you are in total control. Because if you have one foot in yesterday and one foot in tomorrow – you are pissing on today!

When you feel you are under pressure the worst thing you can do is sit still. Make an excuse to get out and swing your arms or go to the rest room and have a good splash in the basin! Breath deep and buy some time to move or attack. But Stoics do not attack, stoics bide their time for the right strategy by using foresight and patience.

So then find the approach which works best for you. Psychologists have now shown that it is nearly impossible to be stressed about another matter when you are exercising. Every time you feel pressure turning into stress, get moving and get breathing and your thinking will start to give you clarity. Studies are revealing astounding results in this area – exercise, exercise and exercise. Or only walk and see your attitude change. If I want to clear my thoughts and have some interesting, creative ideas pop up – I go for a 30-minute walk. If you cannot move, breathe quietly

and deeply and calmness and clarity will prevail.
Shallow breathing is a nasty habit.

Here is a little test to see how your strong lung capacity is at the moment. Take a deep breath and let it out, then do it again. The third time breathe out fully and hold it. Now pinch your nose and hold for as long as you can.

1. 0 seconds – you are in another dimension!

2. 3 – 6 seconds – someone get the defibrillator!

3. Up to 15 seconds – make a doctor's appointment and get yourself checked out

4. 16- 30 seconds – GOYR (get off your rear)

5. 31-40 seconds – you are fit, going well and on track

6. 41-50 seconds – you are nearly at optimum

7. 50 seconds plus – YOU are the programme

If the circumstance of the pressure is spontaneous, deep breathing will immediately cause an intervention and release the neuro chemicals thereby flooding your system with oxygen and adrenaline to make you ready for action and in control. This is a survival mechanism to prepare you for stress or excitement – Now you know a skill to help stop anxiety in its tracks!

What are the greatest virtues of a Leader? – Patience and Foresight. Do you see how these two attributes tie into the above points? When you are being criticized welcome it because it means you matter. The worst criticism you can receive as we now know is to be ignored. **If someone takes the time to tell you how they feel about you this is a blessing thank them and learn.** So, a stoic is a person who is unmoved by externalities, who does not allow their environment, or fears of what other people might think or say about them, determine their mindset and self-worth. **Very good.** So then, let us consider this question, how does a stoic react to criticism? Inevitably you will, be subjected to criticism. Here is a pro-active way you may choose to respond. First give the critic some recognition, to acknowledge that you too are concerned:

*"**Very good.** Thank you very much for telling me I really appreciate it and I am glad you shared with me. Now may I ask you, if I did this from now on would that work for you?"* or *"What do you suggest I should do?"* (Notice I mentioned

you three times in the sentence, use the word **you** as much as you can to build rapport) Responses like above show someone in control and powerful with patience and foresight!

Now what will you do when you do not know what to do?

1. Buy some time by stopping, waiting, quietly take in three deep breaths and say to yourself, "*I am calm relaxed and in complete control.*"

2. Smile wait and do nothing, buy yourself time to think and unpack all the options.

3. Now ask yourself one question; **"What is the right thing to do here?"**

4. Refer to Rule 1 and ask yourself what action here will help me achieve my goals?

5. It is amazing if you just give up the problem to your higher power and wait, ideas and solutions will come, plus in these moments your Mentor can come in handy.

6. No matter what the outcome you will remain indifferent and stoic as that is your nature.

7. If you must act now do so with total commitment and unwavering will.

"Remember between receiving some information and responding there is a gap, a pause, in that moment you have the power to choose your response and in that exceedingly small space lies our growth and to a large degree your success" **-Viktor Frankl.** I have fallen into this trap many times when confronted with a belligerent or aggressive person, I felt the pressure rising, the adrenaline kicking in, the conditioning of the old fight or flight. At that moment I learned to just PAUSE and go within for five seconds and SMILE and BREATHE. Here is a small daily test to start practicing. If feeling challenged or upset by any remark, if you try to avoid or respond you fail the test. When you observe something without reacting you are in total control and you pass. You can feel and appreciate circumstances but remain stoic. You are at a deeper level. This is strength of character.

The point is you are in charge of you. You are responsible for your own actions and to confront yourself all the time is a wonderful way to grow. It is interesting to note every successful person can tell you a story of when they were knocked down flat and then got up off the floor. As the great Boxer Jack Dempsey said, *"A champion is the guy who gets up when he knows he can't."* Mother Teresa the wonderful Nun from Kolkata said, **"Be the person to whom they say; because of you, I never gave up."** No matter what the circumstances, the tide will always turn.

Provided you press on for the right reasons you will win in the end, I give you my word of honour. The best way to build character is through experience. Whatever experience we have is like adding some armour plate to ourselves. When we begin this life, we have little armour other than our voice. As we grow, we build muscle, weight, and height. Plus, knowledge and intelligence.

So, we learn in any task the more we put in, the more we benefit, and the key is to try to put in a little bit more than anyone else. **Every experience good or bad weaponizes us with more protection and capability. Until we become so impenetrable, we feel the pain, but we can still laugh at the world no matter what happens. The ability to endure seems vital. If we do not take up the challenges we do not grow.**

Which makes me think stoicism may have one flaw. Herein a possible example. I had been commissioned by a southern developer to amalgamate an absolute beachfront site comprising a whopping eighteen residences. A site it was believed with too many owners and potential conflicts to redevelop. If successful the properties would then be demolished and a forty story hi rise plonked on top comprising some 150 apartments for me to sell as well as the land sale commission. A mega opportunity! I started in March and soon discovered a top flight lawyer was one of the onsite owners. I thought here was a win win and arranged for him to act for my client the investor in all the transactions. By September I knew every owner by first name and over the back fence" how much did you get?" was the favourite neighbourhood game. I only had a few hold outs to go so doggedly pressed on. But I could tell something was a bit fishy as some of the Options to Purchase were falling due for further payments and my man the developer was running around town trying to find more money even at the horse races find more money, even at the horse races! So, as insurance I acquired one of the last flats and made him the nominated purchaser to protect his and my interest.

Three months later it all collapsed, he turned my recommended *"pit bull"* solicitor against me and my wife and I were woken up at six am one morning with a banging on our door. *"Ray Armstrong!"* *"Not my dog he would never!"*. Wrong answer. A writ was shoved in my hands suing me for a million dollars loss of profit on the letterhead of my own suggested Lawyer. My client never had the capacity to settle on the land let alone fund a massive apartment building. His sole objective was for me to tie up the site and then he would offload the company to a real developer and *clip the ticket* on the re sale for $1 million. Leaving me with no sale and no income for nine months. Thank God my wife was working. Receptionist right next door at the finest apartment complex on the Coast - the forty storey Aquarius. To be eclipsed by this project - in my dreams! I had stoically chipped away as a *"rockbreaker,"* pressing on despite becoming a bit of a joke in the office, through rain hail sleet and now sorrow. In hindsight my error was made on day one PPPPP. I had been on a role from a previous transaction my emotion charged ego was running the show when instead of prior sharpening my axe I was chopping like a mad Royal Show axeman off 24 on the 15-inch standing block. The site collapsed. I saw three lawyers who all went stone cold silent when they knew who they were up against. So, this time I did some belated diligence and upgraded to a genuine *"howitzer"* from the big smoke. Coincidentally our old Rugby Club First Grade Premiership winning Captain. Two weeks later and a few hundred dollars happily paid for one phone call from *my man* it was all over. The Investor forfeited all his borrowed Option funds to the owners, some $300,000 and the site stood there for another forty years.

As Ernest Shackleton said, *"he who endures conquers"*. Know the emotion and show empathy for others pain. Like some people you will meet in life and when you do, they could be a fine friend. Because one cannot defeat the person who stands no matter what, who remains in control and what is more the one with **"Amor Fati"** the one who accepts and even loves their destiny no matter the outcome. This is tough but it is a person who will be respected and who will live a happy and fulfilling adult life. If we do not accept and take up the challenges that befall us, we never grow and realise our own potential.

Lions and tigers do everything in life with purpose and meaning. Ray Lewis US NFL Player stated. *"If a lion is the king of the jungle how can this be? How can a lion be the king if it is not the biggest? An elephant is the biggest. A lion is not the fastest. A cheetah is the fastest and a chimpanzee is the smartest. If a lion is not the biggest, fastest or smartest how can it be the king of the jungle?* **It is because of the way a lion thinks."** –A lion is patient and strategizes then goes all in with savage efficiency and never gives up. Interestingly, to feed herself and the pride it is the lioness who makes 85% of the kills. These too are the qualities of a Paladin Knight from the golden age of chivalry, like the glorious story of Joan of Arc the young peasant girl who was convinced God was guiding her and with great determination led the whole French army against the English in a momentous victory and became a Saint. Are these stories for us to have some sort of belief in ourselves, some sort of faith instilled to stop us from a world of cowardice, selfishness, and chaos? Let us visit that now.

Summary:

- I give everything I do 100%. *"I am not done yet!"* is my mantra.

- I know that the secret to success is really to just keep going - when others stop, I will push on even for one more minute.

- *The problem is always how I choose to see the problem* - Stephen Covey

- When faced with a problem I do whatever I can to fix it if I cannot I accept the situation and move forward.

- I accept outcomes with indifference. I am not moved by outside circumstances, I choose my own reactions and, in this space, I welcome challenges. They are mine to accept and I know my greatest growth will come from my darkest times.

- I laugh often and in the face of adversity I laugh every time because I am a resilient person satisfied in my ability to overcome. Like a Rock Breaker.

- Very good! Every experience is teaching me a lesson, so I welcome these lessons.

- My anxiety is caused by overthinking. If I have done everything I can there is no gain in being anxious or thinking further. Peace is found in acceptance.

- Stop thinking about everything so much. You are breaking your own heart!

- When confronted with a stressful situation I will delay, breathe and exercise.

  - I know the tide will always turn as long as I PRESS ON for the right reasons, endure and do not quit the rewards will come.

- I am the person who never gives up I know pain is coming in life and I accept.

- Your mind must be stronger than your feelings. Every poor decision always comes from emotion rather than your mind. A good splash of cold water works too!

- Sometimes when faced with a difficulty just wait and watch. *Watchful waiting* is even a medical term now in use to see what transpires.

- It takes a lot to offend or upset me - in fact it is almost impossible.

- If you feel exhausted and helpless just give it up to your higher power and have faith

- *"The one who endures conquers"* – Shackleton.

- It's never what happens it's how I choose to react.

- "Define the moment or the moment will define you"- Walt Whitman

ACTION PLAN:

What actions must I do to implement real discipline and intent, what do I do when I do not know what to do? What are my takeaways from this chapter?

1. ....

2. ....

3..

4..

CHAPTER 10

THE BIG QUESTIONS – WHAT'S IT ALL ABOUT?

Firstly, I must disclose I am a Christian, a believer in Jesus Christ, however I believe in the fundamental goodness and unity of all religions.

Varanasi, *the City of Life* whose main business was death. Dawn walking down further, deeper and darker on the so old, worn-down stone steps. In dank narrow laneways which had never seen sunlight that millions of others had trodden and carried their dead family members from time immemorial. The laneways wove between old mantis like buildings in mossy passages which eventually spewed open onto the teeming shore of, *"Ma Ganga"* the mother Ganges River. To the uninitiated it was truly a scene from hell, the huge funeral pyres burn all day and all night and the rancid smell of the dead drifts and mingles together with the sad mourning chants of loved ones. The mantra of those still alive becoming a dream like cadence as the same ceremonies are repeated over and over as they have been for millennia. Even long before Christ was born. Nothing makes one feel so insignificant and reinforces how lucky we are when compared to the benign acceptance of suffering and the apparent happiness of the destitute who seemed to make up so much of the population of amazing India.

It is said life is what happens to you when everything is going exactly according to plan. As you know if you want to make God have a good laugh, tell God your plans!

Our lives can turn on a sixpence. How True! Turning sixteen I was the runt of the litter! Both of my brothers in age, one each side, were six feet plus and my own son grew to six feet three inches. I discovered both my hand me down and hand me up school uniforms were too damn big and being a teenager, this was a catastrophe!

The genesis of this dramatic change in fortune I am convinced started with a family day at the Zoo. I was introducing myself to a camel trying to add some long green weeds to its diet by shoving the shoots in its gob. When in an instant the animal baulked, reared, recoiled the long neck, barked at the sky and as if in disdain and let fly with a massive snort of snot and spittle right in my gob. Two days later, flat on my back in bed, I watched the moon fall from the night sky onto the horizon and become an unstoppable gigantic ball rolling towards me like a humongous, pock marked coconut. I was delirious. Rushed off to hospital and soon unbeknown to me befuddling the best brains in the city's medical fraternity.

The following weeks in an intensive care ward, there I was wasting away like a sun-bleached flathead. The soles of my feet had peeled off, accompanied by blisters all over my body and a tongue so engorged it had transitioned into a blown northwest *"blowie."* The perplexed doctors with no diagnosis, could not administer any effective treatment, other than twice daily shots of anti-biotics for weeks until my legs and arms were literally meaty mince like slabs. Now a bit of a curiosity, the medicos would daily huddle around my bed flipping charts and rubbing chins and subsequently deliver every possible blood and bone test known to man. I am sure some too from books with ancient Latin text! If it ended with an *"osis"* or an *"itis"* it seemed, I had it! Months later I was told on one evening our specialist doctor Ferguson had divulged to my parents I was the sickest person that he had treated in his career, who was still alive. I remember Mum leaving the room in tears, my two brothers mute and lastly Dad dropping his big hand on my shoulder, saying two words I will never forget. *"Be brave."* Say what! How would I do that? I had no idea or control over anything!

I recall late that very evening and to this day I can never be sure if it was a vivid dream or really happening. Waking up to what I thought were a set of spotlights illuminating the entire room. Not *"a posse"* of doctors in white coats again at this hour! No! I was up and about. Well up and above. Still in the room, connected and yet no longer part of the life below. For how long I do not recall, but remember being fascinated, then back into unconsciousness. The experience was etched into my mind. Later I was told the tipping point was that very evening and our family doctor concluded my life saver was all the solitary preseason football training, because I was the fittest I had ever been in my fifteen short years.

Is there meaning of our existence? Is there a divine loving spirit we call God? Is there in fact life after death?

OR: are we; *"A ghost, made of stardust, in a meat covered skeleton, on a rock hurtling through space?"*- Nev Schulman

OR: as the Lebanese Sufi Kahlil Gibran said in death, is it a case of; *"A little while, a moment of rest upon the wind and another woman shall bear me."*

OR: as Norman Greenbaum said with his classic song The Spirit in the Sky; *"I got a friend in Jesus so you know that when I die, he's gonna set me up with the spirit in the sky"*

The above are all viable options. If there is no other choice, well I would then choose to remain happily indifferent knowing I gave this adventure of life my best shot. The fine Canadian actor Keanu Reeves who has had much personal pain in his life was asked by an interviewer, *"What happens after death?"* His response, ***"I know the ones who love us will miss us."***

If you are unsure if there is life after death then you may consider believing you could return to the same place you were before you were born.

You may wish to think about the following examples. Life on Earth happening spontaneously is like being tasked to find one specific grain of sand from every grain in all the beaches, oceans, and deserts of the world. Or if we extrapolated the fingerprint of every person living today and had access to every person who has ever lived for as long as mankind has been here, there is not one fingerprint which would match yours. Could every other creature which has ever existed from insect to elephant also be unique? How could this just be?

These topics have been discussed for thousands of years and still no one knows the answer. There are many suggested conclusions but none proven. However, I would like to share with you some ideas. I read a fable about 100 of the world's greatest thinkers who were informed the answer to this question would be revealed on the top of a great mountain which they each must doggedly climb for years to eventually crawl over the summit and collapse in total exhaustion. Only to find another hundred wise men already there sitting in a circle arguing the same question. No one knows the answer to the big questions so what can we do to give us some clarity?

If we look at the Old Testament with a different lens. There is a definite pattern of messages being delivered by great leaders to create trust, love, goodwill and virtue amongst their peoples. For example one could say Moses saw the persistent disharmony of his tribe and had a cosmic intervention of inspired thought (like Newton, Michaelangelo, Gandhi or Buddha) and wrote the Ten Commandments. But to convince his people he was compelled to say the message came from God. To survive *"forty years"* in the Sinai desert the people learned resilience and the capacity to endure. So he said they were being tested by God. The exodus from Egypt involved infestations of frogs, locusts and flies. Crop failure, boils and a human plague itself. All these things may have happened as the Jewish people were there for 400 years and stories were built to give them credence and that their God had determined they deserved to be freed to return to Canaan their promised land. If we look at all these biblical stories as allegories with messages from sages of how to function best as a society underpinned by goodwill to others the Old Testament stories are a great method of effective management. God is on our side!

For many years, the ABC had a wonderful radio programme called, *"The Spirit of Things."* In one episode the producer and presenter Rachael Kohn explained how a study over many generations had made a most interesting finding. Families and their descendants with two core factors seemed to flourish, and the family line continued to be strong despite many times facing all types of adversity:

A. **Individual virtue (being a good person who does the right thing)**

B. **Group Goodwill (being a person who acts to assist others in need acting with the best interests of all)**

Whereas other perhaps not so gracious families failed to continue their line and disappeared. A most interesting finding. In Rachael's last interview for the programme after twenty-one years studying the world religions and interviewing some of the world's most famous religious leaders, she shared her findings with listeners. Rachael was asked to summarise across all faiths what would be regarded as a successful and meaningful life? In response she quoted an Old Testament passage from the Book of Micah. Micah was a Prophet who stood up for the poor and had the courage to chastise the rich and their worship of idols and desire for material wealth above all, much like some today. Remember at the end of the game of life the King and the Pawn go back in the same box.

Micah 6:8 - *He has shown you, O man, what is good; and what does the LORD require of you, but to do justly, to love mercy, and to walk humbly with your God?*

By that definition what is a good person? My interpretation is that a good person is someone who is morally good in what they do and is fair, who helps and forgives others and is a humble individual. Personally, I have always found the last task challenging, but I will persist as the instruction has come from a most reliable source.

A recent ground-breaking, independent US study of over a thousand children from diverse backgrounds rich and poor over the last ninety years revealed **those who maintained friendships and encouraged close family ties were happier, had less ill health and were living longer.** I know this requires effort you may not want to make for assorted reasons, but all you can do is forgive. I think the best we can do is try to individually live by certain principles which have been shown over thousands of years to deliver a life of relative quality, meaning and happiness. I am no student of world religions but it seems to me in my most limited knowledge and having good friends of each of the following great belief systems Christianity, Judaism, Islam and Buddhism have at their core the same principles, all consistent with Micah 6:8.

So why do most of us struggle to follow the instructions? Are we in fact a human animal striving to survive and become dominant? Remembering the Homo Sapiens dominated, then assimilated all their human contemporaries some 250,000 years ago. Simultaneously proceeding to also eliminate the other flourishing animals, flora and fauna with such ferocity everywhere we have gone we laid waste to the major species in plant life too. And all the evidence says in the history of the planet we are doing a better job of it now than ever before. Make of that what you will, as the resolution to this problem will be up to contributions from you and your children. Who or what are we? So far monsters seems a better fit than saviours?

To help us we may need to seek what gives us a better purpose. So how could one find meaning if one wants to? Soren Kierkegaard the Danish philosopher in his great little book, *"The Lily of the Field and the Bird of the Air"* makes a profound statement from the most widely published and read book in history, the Bible. Kierkegaard says before you pray or worship or develop any relationship with God. *"Seek first the kingdom of God."* Matthew 6: 33.

In the most exquisite book *"The Prophet"* by Kahlil Gibran, when the pilgrim is asked about religion he responds:

"If you would know God, be not therefore a solver of riddles.
Rather look about you and you will see Him playing with your children,

And look into space; you will see Him walking in the clouds, outstretching his arms in the lightning and descending in the rain.

You shall see Him smiling in the flowers, then rising and waving His hands in trees." On Love he said, *"When you have love you should not say 'God is in my heart' but rather 'I am in the heart of God.'"*

GOD IS NOT OUT THERE! Where is the kingdom of God? The Bible says, *"The kingdom of God is within you."* Luke 17: 21. So how does one implement this? We must have faith to draw us closer to God and then we can talk to God through prayer. If one is still and silent and just listens in the moment you may be surprised. I recall being told at school by the visiting Archbishop Reverend Strong to daily recite the following. *"Come into my heart Lord Jesus there is room in my heart for thee."* I still do. You may quietly recite the 23rd Psalm or the Lord's Prayer then you are sending out an invitation to God. **For Christians to win what they seek they must actually give up and surrender themselves to God which seems a total contradiction.** So, by giving in and giving up to God and placing your problems in his hands you become victorious, the scales fall from your eyes and you will see clearly your purpose. Know the right way to live and for your life to have meaning. And it may be very different from what you thought!

Why do we want more and more of what we don't need? A fascinating lesson I have learned is that by giving things away you magically receive. Whenever you give away something that you value it seems the universe rewards you not only with a good feeling but often something else will happen to you right out of the blue many times even more valuable.

If we silently invite the Holy Spirit into us with unconditional love in all our actions that is being honourable, forgiving and humble that means we can be one with and in God. Psalm 46:10 *"Be still and know I am God."* That is no easy task as every single day we will be challenged. But by knowing what we should do we are literally on the journey to the kingdom of God.

1 John 4:16 states, *"God is love, and whoever abides in love abides in God, and God abides in him"*. **So, if the Kingdom of God is within us and if God is love,** that is a life changing statement in itself! And that does not

quite mean going around hugging everyone! In fact, to act with love takes a lot of effort and courage. If you say you love your dog you will take the dog for a walk every day. You will do things for others which require effort without asking. Again, the author M. Scott Peck says in his seminal book The Road Less Travelled - *"Love is the will to extend oneself for the purpose of **nurturing one's own or another's spiritual growth**... Love is as love does. Love is an act of will -- namely, both an intention and an action. Will also implies choice. We do not have to love. We choose to love."* **If it does not require effort, it is not love.** You can get a feeling for God and his love by asking one simple question as situations arise, *"What would Jesus do?"* Indeed, if you practice over following days and weeks you may start to notice changes in your thoughts and actions. Is this the holy spirit welcoming you aboard? It is said, ***"the greatest warrior in the world is the one with the most love in their heart"***.

"To love is to inhabit the energy that can lift mountains and spin planets." That may be a bit of a stretch, but I am sure you get the idea! As the Christian leader Jesus said – **God is Love.** So how do we explain love? Author and lecturer Leo Buscaglia once talked about a

contest he was asked to judge. The purpose of the contest was to find the most caring child. The winner was a four-year-old child whose next-door neighbour was an elderly gentleman who had recently lost his wife. Upon seeing the man cry, the little boy went into the old gentleman's yard, climbed onto his lap, and just sat there. When his Mother asked what he had said to the neighbour, the little boy said, *"Nothing, I just helped him cry."*

If asked, how would you define your feelings towards your Mum and Dad? Or the feeling of loss when you lose a pet very dear to you? I found one simply cannot put love into words. The best examples of love not surprisingly defy description. This quotation from a seven-year-old boy when asked what love is seems to sum it up well, *"Love is what's in the room with you at Christmas if you stop opening presents and just listen."* Love is a verb, a doing word, love requires action and effort. **Love demands courage. Love needs to be demonstrated, *"talk is cheap,"* talk is not love. Real acts of love require action.** As Yvon Chouinard quoted, ***"To do good you actually have to do something."*** Giving of yourself for another is love, the opposite of love is laziness, apathy and selfishness. Love requires you to extend yourself to do something you may find hard to do. Again M. Scott Peck, *"Love is a form of work or courage, if any act is not work or courage it is not love."* It is also said, *"Grief is love with nowhere to go."* - Jamie Anderson. This sad experience will come to you too. This is where the concept of "faith" has a major part to play.

Let us take a step and explore the word *"faith,"* then you are building a potent armament to see you through the grim times. A World War II chaplain said that *"There are no atheists in the foxholes"*. One survey of World War II American enlisted men *"found that the foremost factor enabling them to keep going when the going got tough, was prayer"*. British Army legend, Sir Peter de la Billiere, observed that: *"It is surprising how in war and prison camps, when the future is grim and people are dying, even the toughest serviceman has a reawakening of faith"*. As Alfred Tennyson said, *"More had been wrought by prayer than this world dreams of."* What is this powerful force that compels many of us to seek something beyond any physical capability?

What is faith? Perhaps this story can help explain? A man crossed Niagara Falls on a tightrope pushing a wheelbarrow. When he arrived on the other side he asked the cheering crowd, *"Do you think I can return to the other side pushing my wheelbarrow with someone sitting inside it?"* The crowd shouted, *"Yes, we believe you can!"* He answered, *"Can I have a volunteer?"* Silence no one came. After a while, someone said, *"I will go."* The person who had faith is the one that went. St. Thomas Aquinas said, ***"To one who has faith, no explanation is necessary. To one without faith no explanation is possible."***

When Jesus cured the sick, blind and mad he made the most interesting statement *"I have not cured you, your faith has."* Do you know what he meant? **Faith is a powerful force in all beliefs. It is a key component you need if you choose to believe in a higher power. So, we need faith to draw us to God and then we can become with and part of God.**

I recall an interview with Mother Teresa the Nun from Kolkata the interviewer was confounded pleading, *"How can you possibly believe in God when every day, month* and year you live through the horrors of people dying in front of you from starvation and disease?" The Nun answered in two words, which silenced the entire auditorium. *"Blind faith."* We do not know how it works but we know it does work and involves us making a commitment based purely on having belief and in doing so we open a door to the infinite.

"I do not know if God exists but I do know if I act like he does and follow the pathway offered to us we become closer to knowing what God is." A more compelling statement I do not know.

To summarise we must have the faith to ask God to come into us as the Holy Spirit then believe God is Love. A statement so simple to follow if nothing else, be a loving person and you will be with God. So, can we deduce if God is love and the kingdom of God is within us, if we act with love in our heart we are with and in God's grace?

C.S. Lewis the great English writer summed up in his book Mere Christianity:

"The very first step is to try to forget about the self altogether. You are real, a new self (which is Christ's and also yours, and yours just because it is His) will not come as long as you are

looking for it. It will come when you are on the bottom. Give up yourself and you will find your real self. Lose your life and you will save it. Submit with every fibre of your being, and you will find eternal life. Keep back nothing. Nothing that you have not given away will ever be really yours. Nothing in you that has not died will ever be raised from the dead. Look for yourself, and you will find in the long run only hatred, loneliness, despair, rage, ruin, and decay. But look for Christ and you will find Him, and with Him everything else thrown in."

What a wonderful passage and quite an ask too. Lewis also talks about *"The Moral Code"* inbuilt in all of us from birth knowing what the right thing is to do. **No one is born bad, it takes practice!** Ask yourself in those challenging moments one question. *"What is the right thing to do here?"* It has been said, *"The greatest trap the Devil uses is temptation"*. An example may be a while back I went to the self-checkout register at Coles and found $100.00 cash dangling out of the dispenser. I hesitated, looked around thought, this is my lucky day then knew what I should do. Is that the power of the universe saying, *"Hello"* to you? With many decisions sometimes the best option is to **give it up to God, release the love in you and surprisingly life seems to open for you as never before.**

So could we allow this incomprehensible force to come into our lives, have faith despite all setbacks, remain stoic and when we feel the need give our heart and soul up to God's own determination. Seems a good option based on the experiences of many others.

The son of God, Jesus Christ was certainly no *"wimp"* either. No one pushed him around. He stayed true to his goals, stoic to the very end with values none of us could ever stand alongside. His determination and resilience are all through the New Testament. I know of no man or woman in the history of mankind who ever came anywhere near his example of forgiveness, humility and love. As has been said if you take all the generals in all the armies, all the kings and queens of all the countries, all the leaders and philosophers who ever lived, no one has had the impact on the world as this one young man who *"died"* at just thirty-three. His father giving his own son's life for us in the defining act of grace. By the way if you ever have any doubts about the existence of Jesus and his miraculous story, enrol in an Alpha Course by Nicky Gumble. They are free and readily available worldwide.

I am sure you can see a similar theme, a constant narrative woven into the thread of the conclusions from all these wonderful people. Viktor Frankl the Jewish Psychiatrist, who after surviving a Nazi concentration camp and seeing so many die wrote the worldwide bestseller, Man's Search for Meaning, he concluded the people who generally survived had three traits which I have attempted to sum up as follows:

1. **An objective or a goal had been set even if it was just to survive.**

2. **Love was a driving force, they loved someone, somewhere and they loved them back.**

3. **They were stoically able to rise above the difficulties this life imposed upon them and keep going.**

Again, can you see the pattern? Goal – Love - Stoicism

So, could you embrace the above concepts and instil them into your character? That is a really worthwhile ambition.

Please note for a while I embraced these beliefs to the point where I had changed so much, I was being taken advantage of as some people saw it as weakness,

I became too agreeable and went down a few dark pathways. There was nothing wrong with the concepts as all were proven. My interpretation was wrong. But it then forced me to become truthful and candidly share my feelings with these *"underminers."* Then strangely they seemed to fall away. Perhaps they were exposed and where those who did understand me, respect and friendships blossomed. As they say in Law, *"The truth is an absolute defence"* or as Keats the poet said, *"Beauty is truth, truth beauty and that is all you know on Earth and all you need to know."*

Conversely as opposed to love in other examples I learned to stay right away from some people. M. Scott Peck also concludes the opposite of love is evil which can be displayed by lack of effort or laziness. **He states we must fight against this entropy our whole lives as the truly evil amongst us actively avoid extending themselves. They will take any action in their power to protect their own laziness and contaminate and destroy any person who stays too long in their presence.** Evil is not innate within us, evil is learned.

Yes, I believe I have met and looked into the dead, dark eyes of the smiling face of evil on four occasions. All were oddly similar if that makes sense with questionable past decisions. These people appear to possess the same character traits, corroborated by psychiatrists, albeit under another name - psychopaths:

- Thrilling company as one always knew something was going to happen
- No empathy towards others, no remorse about potential adverse outcomes
- Never accept their own failures and a total denial of any flaws in themselves
- Always looking for the easy way to achieve ends, inherently lazy
- Self-indulgent, desperately proud to look good and appear good
- Control freaks always wanting to impose their poisonous will on others
- Compulsive liars
- I believe evil people cannot comprehend goodness, so watch out for this character flaw in those who refuse to accept our moral code, who act without values and fail to see the good in others

As I learned to distance myself and watch, over time, those who chose to remain close to these people or were locked in, all suffered terribly as if they had been infected by some malady. Eventually the lives of all four of those people too, disintegrated.

I read where a man who had met the demonically inspired mass murderer Adolf Hitler (who eighty years ago tried to take on and defeat the whole of Europe – and very nearly did!). This gentleman said, Hitler saw him in a crowd and fixed on him. Hitler then rushed up and stopped face to face and looked not at him, but seemingly into him with such intensity it seemed as if Hitler was searching past his eyes into his very soul to see if this fellow possessed or the same something inhabited him. One could call it a malevolent spirit. Then appearing disappointed Hitler just stopped and walked on.

I learned to be discerning and aware. Follow my "*mind*" not my emotions and now when I meet someone who I think is always playing the blame game, or a chronic gossiper, or too negative I am on guard. I remember **misery loves company.** Or the worst of all, the pride of the compulsive liar (who incidentally tend to tell the same lies so many times they eventually convince themselves it is the truth). I quietly listen with intent then – well I recall a very important meeting I must attend immediately!

Again, never ever forget, *"If you lie down with dogs you will get up with fleas"* so be careful who you choose to befriend. Because sadly, some will do their level best to make you like them and take you to a place you never want to find yourself.

There are also several luminaries suggesting the age of religion is ending and the world's peoples will and must become the global village to survive. In any case the same principles by different great thinkers advising us over centuries remain true as a guide to life. It seems selfishness is at the core of all our daily problems that gives rise to the second noble truth of Buddhism. Our suffering is caused by our ego, our pride, which drives anger, bitterness, cravings, desires, envy, fear, greed, and hatred. If we watch out for the times when we could be acting selfishly, we may surprise ourselves how often this takes place. In any case we cannot comprehend the meaning of life through *"conceptual thinking"* which is understanding patterns or connections and drawing conclusions irrespective of which belief we choose to follow. The understanding of our existence is outside those realms, in another dimension, found in those quiet still moments such as when we see the sun setting on the horizon or the wonder of a sleeping child.

To transform the above into some form of understanding and to give our life meaning we are well advised to accept the wisdom of those of all denominations before us and therefore **to give our lives meaning depends on what meaning we give our own life,** a good start could be:

1. To set ourselves a goal or a purpose and strive for it with fairness.

2. To try to do the right thing every day by standing with values.

3. To forgive others. As Confucius said, *"He who seeks revenge first dig two graves."*

4. Winston Churchill said to a university packed to overflowing in the shortest and one of the most memorable speeches ever delivered: *"Never, never, never, never, never, never give up."*

5. Be prepared to willingly pay the price of the above, be stoic, find humility and you will win.

6. We must become an unselfish giver not a taker and in doing so our character will blossom.

A fine example which I can relate to of love at work is when one again remembers the actions of Mother Teresa from Kolkata India nursing the *"untouchables."* These souls were the lowest caste or level of community, filthy and sick with disease and no one would go near them, let alone embrace and administer lifesaving help. Mother Teresa when asked how she tendered to them replied, *"Jesus said whatever you do, you do to me."* So, in her eyes is Jesus / a higher power already in all of us?

In the awarding of the Victoria Cross, the requirement is, *"gallantry of the highest order."* Many times, this described men who were prepared to surrender themselves to death and lay down their own life for their friends. US President Ronald Reagan told the story of a Medal of Honour winner during World War 2. A B-17 bomber was returning to its base in England after a raid over Nazi occupied Europe. The plane had been struck by anti-aircraft fire and the ball-turret gunner in the belly of the aircraft had been wounded and was trapped in the wreckage unable to jump. The crew all said their goodbyes and started parachuting out, but as the pilot was supervising the abandonment of the aircraft the imprisoned young gunner who was tragically being left behind cried out in unimaginable fear. The pilot and his second in command returned and sat down beside him. Then the Captain took the young man's hand, ordered the co-pilot to jump and said to the trapped crew member, *"Never mind, son, we'll ride this one down together."* There is only one word to explain this action, the most powerful word in the world, **love and love is when you are with and in the grace of God.** Love is a doing word, it always requires effort and courage to do, not to only say how you feel. John 15:13 one of the greatest statements ever written. To me the ultimate definition of love. *"Greater love has no one than this: to lay down one's life for one's friends."* Interestingly people who live through these and similar horrific episodes, defy death and the few who I have met or worked with or read about or viewed on screen documentaries seem to be the most content and peaceful folk one could ever meet. **Could the pain we endure be a doorway to life's meaning?**

Perhaps if you try to just live according to the previous points you will see yourself subtly changing, others may notice it too? **When grace comes knocking, it is God reaching out his hand to you? Will you take it? So how do you eat an elephant? Just start a bite at a time – an effective way could be today to try to be a little humbler, a little less judgemental and when it arises deny yourself for the sake of others? Grace can be enacted in small actions every day of our lives.**

I have had the privilege of enjoying many of the fine trappings of success, but strangely the best things in life are not tangible, that is things you cannot touch. Warren Buffett said in an interview, *"If you have $100,000 and you are an unhappy person and you think $1,000,000 is going to make you happy, it is not going to happen."* Happiness is about a loving family, one or two faithful friends, knowing yourself and being able to say – *"I think I am a good person."*

Viktor Frankl said. *"The meaning of life is that love is the ultimate and highest goal to which a person can aspire.*

*I grasped the meaning of the greatest secret that human poetry and human thought and belief have to impart: **The salvation of us is through love and in love. I understood how a man who has nothing left in this world still may know bliss, be it only for a brief moment, in the contemplation of his beloved.**"*

We can extend our own relationships by considering our place in the world and our attachment to nature. There appear to be forces at work in this space beyond our comprehension. If you want to explore the fundamental rules of the universe in action, science has now proven, but are mystified by a type of partnering called **Quantum Entanglement. If one atomic particle is split into two then separated and one is deliberately altered even though one maybe here on Earth and the other shot literally into space the other particle involving no speed, no time and irrespective of distance will spontaneously make the identical modification.** As with this phenomenon our method of measurement simply does not exist, even if the particles are separated by millions of kilometres. I urge you to explore the wonder of this marvel. Please note in 1935 Albert Einstein released a paper on the matter but could not comprehend how and why it happens and called it, *"Spooky action at a distance."* How is it so? All substances animate and inanimate may be connected. Carl Sagan the renowned Astrophysicist made the following comment, *"Man is the matter of the cosmos contemplating itself."* Consider why the following examples have the same mathematical sequence in their form. The seeds of a sunflower, our galaxy the Milky Way, a pinecone, a breaking wave, a cyclone, a nautilus shell, the humble egg and every human being. The distance of our shoulder to our elbow being 1 then the distance from our elbow to our fingertips is 1.6. And even the printed pattern of our own heartbeat. This is Fibonacci's Sequence or The Golden ratio. 1+0 =1, 1+1=2, 1+2=3, 3+2=5, 5+3=8, 8+5=13, 13+8=21 and so on. A recurring ratio of 1:1.618. It begs the question should we not consider and respect our planet more and all other living species? Perhaps a good time to take a deep breath say a very long *"hamsa"* (the Buddhist sound of the breath of our life in and out) and thank our lucky stars!

In 1624 some 400 years ago John Donne an English Poet, scholar, soldier and priest said the following amazing words in a sermon: *"No man is an island, entire of itself; every man is a piece of the continent, a part of the main. If a clod be washed away by the sea, Europe is the less, as well as if a promontory were, as well as if a manor of thy friend's or of thine own were, any man's death diminishes me, because I am involved in mankind, and therefore never send to know for whom the bells tolls; it tolls for thee."*

Does this ring any bells about what we have previously mentioned? Could love be a part of the DNA of all existence? Therefore, if we as *"the big bang"* suggests are stardust, all of us are sharing this world together. Would it be a good idea to follow the advice of people like Jesus and do our best towards each other whilst here. How? We could just try to live with Grace and a similarly interesting word from across the sea

Summary:

I think regarding this chapter it is up to each of us to make our own determination. I respect your thoughts to draw your own conclusions about religion, love and a higher power. There is one constant we should remember *"love what you have before life teaches you to love what you have lost."* – Kevin Parikh.

ACTION PLAN:

What actions can I take to help me in my belief system if I choose to have one? How can I overcome my worries and give my life meaning? How can I become a better person and develop my character? How can I be cognizant of people who may be better off to stay away from?

1..
....

2..
....

3..
....

4..
....

CHAPTER 11

MEDITATION AND MANA

"You will attract what you are, not what you want. So, if you want it, then reflect it "– Tony Gaskin

Lahore, Pakistan in the cheapest lodging one could find collapsing into a string bed with the bed bugs and lice as the ever-inquisitive scurrying rats lolled me off to sleep.

From Delhi travelling third class by train, packed like, well a third-class Indian train, full of the friends of the Punjab with their ducks and baby goats all on board. After literally head down *"ruckie"* hitched high, hitting the carriage doorway like one smashes into a rugby ruck to eventually cleave my way on board I had to then try to stay awake all night. I felt like and was a real outsider. Oddly I never saw any other westerners in third class and the whole carriage was always full to beyond capacity, complete with people even travelling on the roof! Occasionally I would be startled as one roof rider, held upside down by a mate would miraculously appear shaking his head and grinning at me through the window. One hand happily clinging to the iron security bars and the other wildly reaching out at me, maybe hoping the smoke from the old *"puffing billy"* locomotive would disguise his pickpocketing. Inside casting around and seeing many of my fellow travellers hypnotically swaying staring at me. I was convinced they were willing me to sleep so they could have a quick *"whip around"* with my now most frugal possessions. I can still remember glaring back at my imagined adversaries with the most malicious intent I could muster, hearing the remorseless tunka, tunka, tunka and sway of the train and feeling so very alone. Whilst my fellow passengers looked so content, living in the moment seemingly happy with their lot and always alert for any opportunity that may present itself!

How is it that millions of the poorest in this world can live with such acceptance? Meditation and mindfulness are taking the world by storm. They are however slightly different – in meditation the goal is to think of nothing, while in mindfulness the goal is to focus – be aware or mindful – of something. I try to use both for a similar purpose, so I will talk about them together.

Is their current popularity a good thing? I think it is. We all must slow down a bit and that concept fits in perfectly to the kind of person we all would wish to be. Meditation helps you reset, recalibrate and recharge. But it is hard to master perhaps like much else in this book but easy once you practice.

I have tried the technique for years and mostly seem to drop off to sleep or remember something I had just forgotten which was not important and not urgent and go and do it! So, we accept meditation is not easy. That is probably one of the reasons it is good for you. But remember now you have accepted that it is not easy it will become easier. If you want to see how much stuff is going on in your mind just stop, let your shoulders slump, **allow your tongue to fall from the roof of your mouth,** close your eyes **and focus on focussing on nothing only breathing.** Try for only one minute and just be at peace.

There is a Buddhist expression called *"sweeping the temple"*. When the monk is sweeping the temple, they are doing and thinking of nothing else!

This is one of the most worthwhile skills one can learn in life. When you are doing anything 100% focus on the task that is the key. When you are just sitting alone try to focus your entire being on being there still and your mind at peace.

Most of us lose concentration too easily and drift off to Someday Isle. A good exercise which a Hindu friend recommended to improve your concentration and relax. Breathe in deep and breathe out only through your mouth saying OOOOOOO until you run out of breath. Then breath in again through your nose and closing your mouth breath out through the nose and make a humming sound like HHUUMMMMM. This is difficult as you may keep wandering off. Practice until you can stay mindful of only the actions for one minute then three and longer. I am confident your powers of concentration in all aspects will improve considerably. **You are training your mind to stay in control of what you tell it.** For example, when trying to hit a golf ball, shoot a netball or sitting an exam. If you have trained yourself to maintain this type of focus you may be surprised at the increase in your ability to stay focussed and hopefully deliver more positive outcomes. Practice this daily and see the benefits on achieving the objective unfold in calm focus. Great when reading questions or looking into problems.

In meditating, unlike our Buddhist friends I cannot say *"Hamsa"* (the word which sounds like your breath in and out) 100 times let alone 10,000 times a day or *"Om mani padme hum"* 5000 times in a row. Instead, I suggest you find a simple meditation like, *"This is good for me"* or *"I am calm and relaxed and in complete control"* or the one I was taught at school, *"Come into my heart Lord Jesus, there is room in my heart for thee."* Repeat whilst slowly breathing in then out, pausing for a second, then repeating. When practicing at the pause, before you take the next breath this moment is supposedly sacred and the core of your being. So be mindful of this moment in time. Then just keep slowly repeating the breaths or the mantra. The hard part is to stop thoughts entering your mind. When this happens just say to yourself, *"OK thought, I got it, now go away"* and come back to your breathing. You must keep trying and you will be surprised how calm you can become. You may also notice how busy and demanding your mind is on *"stuff"* of no consequence right now - like, *"Where did I leave those damn bongos?"*

I am certain you will feel the difference. Or be with your higher power in a prayer or be with God in silence. Even whilst looking at the amazing beauty of a single leaf. These are techniques you can use anywhere, anytime and you can, for a moment in time – JUST BE.

I also found it humorous and perhaps a bit revealing about some of us, evidence discovered from a controlled test in Science magazine. The test supervisors firstly gave all participants in the exercise a jolting electric shock. Then sat each down alone in a blank four walled laboratory room for fifteen minutes in which they could push a button on the table in front of them and receive the same shock again, if they chose to do so. The results were startling. Even though all participants had previously stated that they would even pay some money to avoid being shocked with the electricity, **67% of men and 25% of women chose to inflict it on**

themselves rather than just sit there quietly, think and BE. Some of us fidgets, cannot even for a fifteen minutes just sit and be!

Meditation is a way to take control of the way you want to live your life and in fact it is remarkably similar to prayer. As has been said, *"Be still and hear God."* The same peace can be found by just giving yourself up to God's will. How do you do that? It is a wow type of feeling. All you do is keep it simple and do not over think it. You could just say *"God this is too much for me, I give up I will place this matter in your hands and **I surrender to your will.**"* When you do this and commit yourself, something inside you seems to know. One could say you are connected or *"plugged in"* to a power source far greater than we ever knew. There would have been many times in my life when I was in such a situation and surrendered to God with all my heart and had faith in his will. I can promise you I have never been abandoned.

Meditation or prayer even for just one minute should be a part of each of our daily lives, as it works! If I can just push away all the stuff I always seem to be dwelling on for a few minutes and **be in that moment,** it is energising as you **feel you may be a part of something greater.**

However, the secret is a bit like exercise, use it or lose it. If you do not practice only for one or five minutes daily it is gone. **The benefits a small amount of time gives you back in clarity and peace are so worthwhile.** Try anytime during the day to sit and stop and – BE IN THE MOMENT. A wonderful way is to look around and take in the living world around you as you start to feel part of nature itself. Or one of my favourite meditations is a sound exercise; go outside, close your eyes and listen to all the noises present. You never actually hear these subtle sounds until you are truly silent and after a few seconds **for just a moment you will be,** *"in the moment,"* exactly where you need to be in meditation. You will be in the present, not thinking about yesterday or tomorrow or this afternoon. I find it so relaxing in letting it all go for a moment, it is rejuvenating. Try this little test by Eckhart Tolle. *"Sit down close your eyes and be silent* and ask yourself 'I wonder what my next thought will be". Then become very *alert like a cat waiting for a mouse to come out of a hole."* It may take a moment but, in that moment, you are free of thought and you are

293

in the moment. How long did you last? A few seconds? If so, may I suggest you need to take your foot off the pedal!

If you can do this and find peace and keep practising, you are, in a way opening a corner of the universe or the *"space time continuum."* Trust me you are going fast in the right direction and not even moving, as in that moment you may be feeling God within you. Or otherwise, you could be with Marty McFly in the *"flux capacitor!"* The meditations above only require you to sit, ideally in an upright position with feet on the floor (please do not lie down as if you do, this is a wonderful way to fall asleep) and practice. Meditation is all about being in the present for a few moments. Not easy but perhaps that is why they call it. *"The present."* Remember, the key to successful meditation is to be patient and persistent. It may take some time to get the hang of it, but with regular practice, meditation can become an invaluable tool for reducing stress and promoting inner peace. **Do not forget worry is paying interest on trouble which has not and may never even happen. You are no longer a worrier you are a stoic and meditation fits in perfectly with stoicism.**

Let us now visit this curious word, **Mana**. Herein a definition of a Paladin, which is remarkably similar to that Polynesian word Mana. *"The knight is a person of blood and iron, someone familiar with the sight of smashed faces and the ragged stumps of lopped-off limbs; they are also a demure, almost a maiden like, guest in hall, a gentle, modest, unobtrusive being. They are not a compromise or happy mean between ferocity and meekness; they are fierce to the nth and meek to the nth"* - C.S. Lewis

Mana rhymes with banana but do not ever say that! One of my good old friends is Brian a New Zealander. His parents separated when he was only eight and he and his siblings were doled out to relatives. He left school on his fifteenth birthday, having attended twelve different schools! But Brian pressed on. He earned the great appointment of being selected to represent New Zealand in the Rugby League World Cup but missed out due to injury a week before the tour left for overseas. He was again selected the following year, however, Brian had only recently married Gail (his wife now of 52 years) so chose not to accept the honour. Later Brian was chosen to play for the North Sydney Bears in I believe the toughest team sport in the world, the Sydney Rugby League competition. His position, Front Row the home of the *"dark arts"* where everything nasty always started and as we were told by our own Rugby coaches, where every game was won or lost. He played against some of the game's greatest, going *toe to toe* with legends like John Sattler who played seventy-eight of eighty minutes of a grand final with a broken jaw! Brian often stunned commentators into silent awe with his courage and all this whilst he was only twenty-two! After leaving North Sydney, Brian represented NSW Country and by coincidence played against a New Zealand touring team. Brian and I worked together for some years. He would be in the office every day at 8am and no one offered more commitment. He was, to look at, a big hard man and yet on meeting him he was one of the most considerate, genuine, real people I have ever had the privilege to call a friend. We used to train together to run the marathon and do not forget he was a big bloke, so that required much more determination than many of us lightweights who choose the endeavour of the forty-two kilometres. Plus, to care for his family he trained whilst holding down two jobs. This was years ago and of course due to his discipline and character he became highly successful in business too. Retired now, Gail and Brian now live in a luxury apartment in Cronulla, Sydney. He told me recently he was hit smack in the head with an errant golf ball from a player some ten metres away, which caused some serious bleeding. His companions said, *"We better take you back to the club and call an ambulance."* Brian's response was, *"No I will see out the game,"* and jokingly he told me he even parred the last hole. **A most remarkable man with a fascinating way about him, life had been so hard, and yet he was so kind. Brian said the best piece of advice he could offer to anyone was – ACCEPT and ADAPT.**

I noticed one night when I was coaching the U15's there was another chap in the WA Rugby club who stood out like a beam from a lighthouse. He had the look and demeanour of one would imagine, a time travelling *Viking* - bred of blood and tradition. He was a Māori, much taller than those half a dozen around him, who were too, all big men. This *"south sea Viking"* was in control, watching and always feeling the tempo of the club environment. He was long limbed, rangy, but muscled up, with a jaw like one sees after many years of *"facing it."* The haircut quite unlike anything I had ever seen, it was a Mullet at the back but very short on the sides and spiked on top but not too long it could be grabbed. This bloke was designed to be you could say *"open for business"* at all times. He commanded a corner of the place where I noticed he could see the whole room but still had about two metres behind him to the wall where I also noted no one was seated. I asked my friend who is that *"big kahuna?"* And he said jokingly, *"That's Joe. He used to play outside me in the Centres, he just appeared one day from NZ and very quickly set a no-nonsense standard we had never seen before. No one would ever mess with him then and nothing has changed. In fact, he took the whole club with him to another level."* I could tell by his presence, he was a *"lion"* and just as dangerous. The way he gave me the up and down – which lasted only about a second, then totally discounted me as no one of significance, was a bit disconcerting too! I met Joe again a few months later, face scarred up, leg in plaster, on crutches. He had a shocking motorbike accident and was lucky to be still with us. But there he was larger than life, again laughing, with an admiring group around him, we managed to have a quick yarn. **The same aura**

of light and energy were again apparent to me in those few minutes.

In Sydney, chance offered me another opportunity to explore this personality type. At a major hotel I met a genuinely nice, exceptionally large Māori doorman trained in, *"conflict resolution."* After chatting for a while, I felt comfortable enough I could open up a little to him. I mentioned, over the years through Rugby and friends I had met a few fellow Māori. But what intrigued me, was some seemed to possess this calmness and inner peace, yet still had a presence of shall we say, pure *"hard eye"* terrible force. I was asking this big *"fella"* was I imagining things or what was this powerful energy I sensed together with genuine humility? He had a laugh and quietly said, *"You white guys do not even have a word for it."* Now I was really interested! I realised I had always been onto something. I asked him very nicely would he care to elaborate, elucidate, or spill the beans? Whilst I leaned slightly forward, looking intently, with a smile and my head slightly turned to the left.

He then said, *"We never even discuss this word out of respect, it comes from our ancestors and is sacred to our people."* So, he wrote it down on his hand. The word was MANA.

In his outstanding book, *"Legacy"* James Kerr wrote about the All-Blacks Rugby team the most successful sporting team of any type in history with a 78% winning average. The author states, *"Mana captures many qualities, authority, status, personal power, bearing and charisma. Mana is perhaps the ultimate accolade, the underlying spiritual goal of personal existence."* Others have argued that it is the universal life force that is the very origin of our ideas of God. Certainly, it describes a person of rare quality; a natural leader possessing strength, leadership, great personal power, gentleness – and humility. **When asked about Chris Ashton, the English rugby winger and his habit of swan diving for a try, former All Blacks Captain Anton Oliver said, *"If one of us did that we'd just die."***

The All-Blacks Richie McCaw who many say was the greatest Captain and Rugby player of all time is a definition of Mana. Back-to-back World Cup wins, 148 games for his country and led the team to the highest average win rate of any sporting team in history. A quiet, stoic, authentic man (spare time a pilot in the New Zealand Airforce) when he left school at eighteen, he wrote on a small paper napkin a list of his goals which he pinned on a curtain in his room. He achieved everyone including the last goal on the list, the letters GAB (Greatest All Black).

*(Now may I ask if you are **not** a Māori or Pacific Islander just be respectful here, please do not use this word or abuse it in any way).* I know this may sound a bit *"wacko"* but **I am convinced some people do have a purity of life force** which can simply attract one to be in their presence. These rare Māori men and women I had the privilege of meeting over the years seemed to, *"shed light"*. Perhaps we could all aspire to have such a word quietly attached to us one day?

I have met a few similar people who were not Māori. Jonas was one, another my boss at Australia's largest pastoral company. Again, a man who was one of the *"tunnel rats"* who actually dug part of the World War 2 tunnel to escape the Germans, from where the movie,

"The Great Escape" was derived. Dr. Geoff Cornish was a heart specialist and one of the most down to earth, generous, genuine people I have ever known. What is this inner strength which makes these people seem to *"shine"* and underpins their humility and character?

Over the years I attended many motivational functions with guest speakers, many of whom were rated as the world's best in their fields. At one talk I attended, the Speaker was a local Australian Hockey player called Rechelle Hawkes. Rechelle's outstanding record speaks for itself, but her character shone in her story. Her physical training in preparation for the Olympics was unlike anything I had ever heard or read in any Australian sport. The demands on her leadership and the sheer power of her personality were such that when I left the room I was totally inspired and humbly in awe of this woman who gave so much. Rechelle won three Olympic gold medals, two as Captain of the Australian team, won two World Cups, five Championship Trophies and a Commonwealth Games title making her the most successful woman to ever play the game. In fact, to me Rechelle Hawkes stood with very few on the podium of all the speakers I have heard across all sectors including the international business fraternity. So strong and yet so humble, with an unmistakable *"Mana"* in her character.

The nub of what I am saying is these people all possessed the same intrinsic something and they were not longwinded about conveying it. They could get to the point quickly and effectively, sometimes without even saying a word, just a presence.

These were resilient human beings, who had suffered, with big doses of determination and stoicism but still the best to share a laugh with and enjoy the moment.

You knew they meant what they said and again **there was never any grey in values. You were either in or out, a good person or not. There were no shades of colour. It was black or white in everything they said and did. You see they knew what was right and they knew and tried to do the right thing every time, so decisions were not hard, they just required some courage.**

You do not have to be a champion to live this way, but we can just try to follow their lead. I try and it sure works – there is no grey, **if you think you may be doing the wrong thing – you are!** When you adopt this stoic sort of attitude, you grow as a person and do not stop. You will attract people to you because they just want to be part of what you have. I now realise I was so privileged to have made the effort and met these fascinating, good Paladins. Today's knights with another form of armour - Mana. We, of other heritages

Summary:

- Meditation or quiet prayer is a life skill which should be learned and implemented daily.

- The ability to just "be" in the present, in the moment, is a powerful state that pays dividends. Every day take some time to just breathe.

- I will practice two-minute meditations to train my mind to focus so I can apply to the subject at hand and in doing so increase the probability of success.

- There is the Observer and the *"what if's* when you feel this influencing your mind STOP recognise it is your pride and discard.

- The quiet confidence and stoicism people of honour and many champions possess is a character skill to be developed day by day.

- Mana is earned by being the quiet humble person who WILL act in the face of fear.

- I know right from wrong there is NO grey I try to do the right thing every time so life becomes easier.

- When things dramatically change. I ACCEPT then ADAPT. If I must stand alone, I will that is how I am.

ACTION PLAN

What do I need to do to develop my ability to be mindful and someone of substance?

How will I practice the art of meditation?

1..

....

....

....

....

....

How can I develop my form of Mana?

2..

....

....

....

....

CHAPTER 12

VALUES- STANDING UP - I AM ACCOUNTABLE

"What does it mean to have grace in your heart?
It means gracefully letting things go that are not meant
for you. It means going beyond your inclinations of
trying to get the upper hand or revenge on someone
who hurt you. Having grace in your heart and soul is
choosing to be the person who gives."

Greece, up past the heroic stand of the Spartans at
Thermopylae then heading north and east to the Golden
Horn. I started strolling into this antique city then
stopped dead confronted with a view and sounds from
another time. The East. Another world and one of the
world's greatest cities - Byzantium / Constantinople /
Istanbul. A citadel which over hundreds of years, as the
prize of the world had endured massive sieges with
catapults, battering rams, bows and arrows by Attila the
Hun, Crusader Knights, Mongol hordes and the

Ottoman Turks themselves. The gateway to the orient. I remember being struck immediately by the seeming denser air, the cacophony of noise and the seemingly sad lament of the calls to prayer five times a day. Indeed, another world. I wandered awestruck through the Blue Mosque and then down and I mean down to the amazing Grand Bazaar. 2500 years old, 4000 shops over sixty-four streets and all under the ground. Where one could buy gold, myrrh, frankincense and anything else a person could desire! I was minding my own business foraging in various little stalls for any ancient nick-knacks. When a smiling Mustapha dropped a big *"mit"* on my shoulder and whispered, *"Effendi you are seeking a genuine antique bracelet from the era of the knights templar!"* Amazing, exactly the sort of antiquarian relic I had been rummaging around for hoping to get lucky. I asked how much and he responded with an even larger smile, *"Just the knife, man!"* *"What knife?"* *"The one in your jeans pocket."* Now his smile, a malevolent snarl. Previously in Naples Italy wandering some back streets I ended up in a little store and on sharing the fact that I was destined for Turkey and beyond the salesperson recommended a large ivory flick knife would come in handy. Somehow, somewhere I must have earlier taken the *"brute"* out of my jeans pocket and the word had spread. Walking backwards laughing and denying any such knife existed I bumped smack into the chest of Abdullah the Butcher from WCW and his offsider The Undertaker. All I can recall is spinning like a Dervish then bolting between the two big lumps running as one only can in pure terror, up the arcades until eventually above ground again and then around in little circles until the shock wore off. Later I was strolling along explaining my encounter to a fellow traveller who I had linked up with, when crack right on the face. I was being slapped by my companion, previously a cute, demure damsel. I was accused of not being cognizant of the locals attempts at pinching, grabbing, sliding, leering and generally pawing her for the past hour! She was ostensibly in my care and I had no idea I had entered a completely different culture. Next day solo again.

You will inadvertently let others down. In fact, do not ever think everyone is going to like you. We are biologically designed to be rejected by some, this is nature's way of tactfully telling us this relationship will not work. So, accept it, move on and know we simply are not and will not be a good match. The *"different drummer"* concept in action again. Linda Ronstadt's great song Different Drum about telling a boy to *"back off"* sums it up well:

"So, don't get me wrong it's not that I'm knockin"
It's just that I am not in the market.
For a boy who wants to love only me....
Yes, and I ain't sayin" you ain't pretty.
All I'm saying's I'm not ready for any person.
Place or thing to try and pull the reins in on me, so Goodbye,
I'll be leavin'
I see no sense in this cryin' and grievin'
We'll both live a lot longer if you live without me."

I am sure that explains why my ability to secure females phone numbers was around one in thirty. My drum or their drum was always playing a different war dance! Yet some opposites do attract, because scientists tell us we have learned over thousands of years an innate feeling for what we need to make us better people than we are now. So sub-consciously we are seeking other beings that will improve us all the time, consequently we may like a complete opposite and they you. If that is the case trust me that person is giving you something you need and could be a great friend or even

310

more. Also, you may want to like someone else but they know / feel you are not good for them, so they push you away all the time. That is OK too. You will know the difference in your heart, as do not forget *"love does conquer all"*. Love is the most powerful force in the universe.

So, we all must remain stoic and accept our disparities - *"viva la difference"*. The same may be said of our own values.

There is an old joke, *"See that fellow he thinks ethics is a place in England."* Of course, it is a play on words with an English county called Essex. You must hold the line in every situation, being an ethical person and grow accordingly. Sometimes you will be tempted to do something which is not right so perhaps you can be better liked or to improve your position. How do you know it is not right? The little voice called your conscience that you must live with knows, because the amazing thing is we have all grown up knowing intrinsically right from wrong - a bit like individual virtue. If you want respect, you will need to act bravely at some time. In fact, it may only take one act to create a reputation that will stand for a long time. The same spontaneous single wrong act can destroy a reputation.

The office management had arranged a game of Paintball for all the staff, to build up team morale. The event was held out in the bush. We split into two teams including administration, sales and management. One team had to assault what we were told was a fort. It looked more like the aftermath of a three-day music concert with palings askew, sprung boards and paint in every possible colour splattered all over the place. Whilst the other team sorted out their attack strategy, we defended the ramparts of our fortress. I was assigned to defend a three-legged wooden tower. Our defence was going well but the fear of raising your head to take a shot was terrifying. I recall the commanding officer of the SAS Regiment once told me the most important thing in infantry combat situations is to, *"hold the line of fire"*. This means, being the one to potentially expose themselves to the enemy and make sure if they raise their head, it is you who has the shot. I tried it once earlier in the day. Too late! My peek around cost me splattered goggles and a noggin very like a split red watermelon!

On the other team was Kathy from administration. A quiet, introverted secretary whose attire was always like her demeanour, most feminine and discreet. Her overall attitude for any office duty was. *"The answer is yes, now what is the question?"* We were all surprised she even showed up. Kathy was a devout Christian, whose Dad was a minister, and we were often embarrassed if any of us said OMG in her company.

After about twenty minutes which seemed to me like two hours, the assault from *"the barbarian horde"* was dying, repelled at every charge, the day was ours. They and us all knew it, except one. From cover, one of the beaten blue overalls had suddenly launched - one out! Yes, it was our own Kathy sprinting to the fort entrance and unloading upon us with *"Jason Bourne"* accuracy. I ducked, head glued to the floorboards. Two of our bravest defenders, both hard cases in the credit control department were wiped out and then with single minded determination quiet Kathy *"the Terminator"* focussed on my now shaking, little Tower. I already had my arms halfway up, when Kathy decided not to take any prisoners, shot to pieces with pink paintballs from directly under my open escape hatch. This shy, good woman gave the rest of her team the courage to attack, and we were obliterated. From that moment on Kathy was admired, respected, and treated with a certain amount of caution! A quiet willing worker in the office who always stepped up when asked the question. Character and determination hidden until called into action.

The opposite also applies. Sometimes you will be requested or prompted or cajoled to do some dumb things. Indeed, you may be familiar with the term, *a rite of passage.*" In many societies there are traditions transforming our young into adults, some quite scary. In our communities we have also established some of our own, shall we say quirky rites, which deliver anything but a transition to an adult. We had a few in the surf club like burying someone up to their neck in the sand and leaving them alone on the beach for an hour or so. Until the day one member was nearly run over by the beach inspectors 4WD! You may wish to be somewhat circumspect when preyed upon to perform "a *rite of passage*" by associates. **As a leader and a stoic, you are always in control of your emotions and do not**

fall for childish nonsense, which could easily incur a very heavy, in some cases, lifelong penalty. Hold the line, stand alone and be stoic. Warren Buffett - The Oracle of Omaha said, *"the most successful people say NO relentlessly because they are non-distractable from their mission."*

Your character is always being tested. If you join the *"pack"* and go with it, then when it all goes wrong, you wonder why you did go along? As you knew from the very beginning because you were quietly told by your most trusted advocate, yourself - this was the wrong thing to do. If you do choose to join in, just watch out for the price you may pay for the supposed rite of passage.

In being challenged there is another addictively tempting adversary in the 21st century - computer games. This billion-dollar industry has caught the world in its vast net and few escape. Designed, often by teams of psychologists to keep people playing by activating their mental synapses, releasing dopamine and hooking the users like addicts. Then rewarding users with incentives to secure *"protection"* and requesting monetary contributions to quietly bleed players dry. I know examples of young men and women in their thirties who are aware they are expending their entire disposable income every week on gaming and resigned to it. These games or as Eckhart Tolle refers to them are, *"mental viruses."*

In a city in Saudi Arabia it was revealed there were 4000 scammers in one building! A cohort of these people utilising You Tube! These predators even had a name for their activities, ***"pig butchering"***. Initially offering small payoffs and or building relationships, enticing the victims by larger returns and then draining all their savings or blackmailing them. As one offender stated, *"We find a piglet, fatten them up and then butcher them"*.

Studies show that gaming and too much social media involvement can drive participants towards anxiety, isolation, relationship breakdowns, negative thought habits and poor physical health due to lack of exercise. Our minds are so cluttered with devices demanding our attention that we lose our ability to relate to reality. Indeed, there are cases of adults so compelled to keep playing they wear nappies - so they do not have to go to the toilet! You must look at yourself and know when enough is enough. Get up, take a walk outside and reset your priorities. How much gaming is considered suitable? **Sixty minutes a day maximum! As to social media involvement and banter. Same.** Ask yourself one question who will benefit from this post? In receiving negative posts, you become what you think about. So, will you choose to be a victim, a fool or a leader? Do not post negative detrimental comments try to be pro-active. Have a laugh at negative feedback and move on.

It is always nice to be asked. Or is it? A few times in my life I have experienced interesting propositions. The first in Darwin when I was living at a new work friend's place with a couple of other acquaintances, both into hard drugs. Incidentally on their way to India, where I had recently returned. I noticed both were quite lazy and neither worked. As I used to jog off to my job as a labourer, they would be bending another spoon and cooking up their *"fix"* for the day. Resulting in both on the carpet, smiling a crooked grin as I went out the door. On arriving home, there they were, poleaxed still on the floor. Unmoving, staring like a koi fish when taken out of a pond and placed on the pavers, their back against the wall, nodding, oblivious to the world. When *straight* they were engaging guys, who continually elucidated the wonders and exhilaration of this out of world experience, urging me to try, just once. The temptation was hard to resist.

The second time it was a bribe of a new Mercedes Benz. I had amalgamated six old beach houses for acquisition and demolition by a Melbourne developer and I was marketing the entire sixteen storey building of sixty-five apartments. The Architect who had won the contract to design and supervise the building and I had put forward as the recommended candidate was a personal friend. I was asked by the owners of a carpet company if I subtly leveraged my relationship with the architect to give their firm the contract to lay the floor coverings, there was a new Mercedez Benz in it for me and they would still be the best quote. The Architect was and still is a valued friend. His firm had won the design and construction business entirely on their own merit.

The third involved shall we say an acquaintance from *"the dark side"*. Yes, I had breached my own values too, by being drawn in with his group. A great person to hang out with and after a time being introduced to his friends, a fine bunch of seemingly wealthy, happening guys. Then I witnessed the power of the wolf pack and evil at play. **Do not forget, *"If it walks like a duck, looks like a duck and quacks like a duck it is probably a duck."*** -Walter Reuther

In the first predicament it was morbidly fascinating as I could see these acquaintances slowly being eaten alive from the inside. Like being *"fly blown"*. Their bodies and minds disintegrating when all they could see were days of blissful ennui. I kept delaying the *"one go"* despite both eventually calling me every name - except my own! In a matter of a month the horrible transformation was complete, and I knew I had made the right decision.

The second was a temptation initially but I could not live with myself as someone would have had to pay for the vehicle, plus now I could be bought.

As to the third a few hard **No's** finished that relationship very quickly. In retrospect those *"exciting"* people I know of in the third category, most are now inside, insane or in the ground.

So, my values were tested, and I found a great new strength from these decisions and strangely it became easier to reject and say no along the road in life to potentially so many wrong choices. I knew somehow, I was becoming a more resilient, vigilant person within myself and did I dodge many bullets just by saying a hard NO! Now I may be a bit extreme but when I see a too easy, even fun opportunity coming my way, I just remain indifferent, smile and then politely disappear!

The values I had learned to embrace were, I could be trusted to keep my mouth shut if told something in confidence. I would never steal anything as once you do *"lift"* something not yours I am reliably informed you will want the payoff again and you will do it again. **I ask myself what is the right thing is to do in challenging instances and not act emotionally?** I try extremely hard not to tell lies or if that seems the only option, I choose to say nothing. Sometimes I break, for example when one of your friends asks, *"Do you like my new hairstyle? It is called the pink flamingo?"* **One of my favourite responses to any question I wish to answer without answering is to say with a smile.** *"You may very well say / ask that, however I could not possibly comment."* I would reach out to support a friend always, no matter what had happened. I tell myself daily, love requires action not talk.

Those are my values only, they are not hard to live by if you keep them at the front of your mind. Of course, it becomes easier as your standards become embedded as your values and you are becoming a Leader. But you will be challenged repeatedly and of course you will fail repeatedly but every time you do you will have learned something. **Because if you do not accept and adapt you will repeat the mistake / lesson over and over,** until something really bad happens which you may regret for the rest of your life. **Plus, you now have an objective, and nothing must get in your way. Distractions are just an annoyance to you and to your determination to reach your target. You are happiest when your life has meaning and that is when**

you have a goal and when your values go to work to help you arrive at that goal.

I recall a few situations when for twenty years I had the privilege of offering my services to two of the country's most iconic companies. Both I think are good examples of the calibre of the management and the business strategies of who you may choose to offer your services. One was an airline and my job was sourcing business back from top clients we had lost due to unknown factors. One of these clients a massive European multinational had specialised drilling machinery which needed shipping urgently across the country. As breakdowns in the mining industry could cost hundreds of thousands a day in lost production, I quoted our premium service at an appropriate rate to provide the service required. The State Manager became aware of this significant transaction and on becoming cognizant of the urgency factor instructed me to call back the client and load up the price by another 100% due to *"a lack of space on the aircraft!"* The product had been weighed, allocated space, approved and ready to be loaded. He knew the client, now due to time constraints had no other options. Shocked I told him we

322

already had negotiated and agreed on a price and the deal was done. However, the *"big boss"* reinforced his orders. Dismayed I accepted his instructions, but suddenly found myself busy on another matter altogether.

The original transaction went through, and all went well, with the client eventually becoming again one of our top accounts. The question is, was our State Manager just maximising the company's financial opportunities as he should? Was this method of business systemic in the company management? For me, the group goodwill and individual virtue seemed questionable. Or by not following instructions did I contribute to potential drops in profitability? That great Australian airline, which was literally a household name, sadly no longer exists.

You too will have your values called into question at some stage and you will have to decide as to the benchmark you will be prepared to accept and to live with that decision.

Whilst appointed at another iconic Australian firm with a 180-year-old history we were embarking on a new venture of offering country property franchises (independently owned offices who would use our name). My brief was to grow the Franchise business in the regions through facilitating best practice applicants only. After some weeks I started negotiations with a potential candidate and our diligence suggested we should proceed. Part of the Deed of Agreement included an exclusive territory which would be the franchisees alone to develop and all leads which came out of it would go to his business. The territory covered a good area bounded by a highway and a shire zoning. We all agreed and were ready to sign off when the client asked me to extend the southern border to a railway line to make it easier to manage. I mentioned we already had a deal, but I was excited by this opportunity. I explained the situation to the State Manager and he smiled at me saying, *"Well, we had an agreement beforehand and now he wants to change it, is that right?"* I said, *"Yes sir."* He asked me what I thought. I advised it was not too unreasonable, so he agreed on my recommendation.

Then we had the agreement re-drafted and a week later presented again to our client for signing. He was happy, but just before signing off asked could we not just stretch this side boundary out to the river to make the territory a nice formal shape easily understood by all? He then insisted I put the new proposal forward. I understood his logistics and after a couple of days of mental preparation, a few strong coffees and on the odd occasion the State Manager passed my office told, *"the quiet man"* how fit and well he looked. I made an appointment and ventured up to the offices with a view, carrying a brown paper bag a vanilla slice for the all-knowing personal secretary, who always saw through my feigned bravado. Perhaps the cold sweat on the forehead was a give-away?

On being buzzed in by *"the Gatekeeper"* I explained it all to the State Manager who was quite succinct in his response, *"Fine, tell him no."* I was a little bit surprised but accepted his decision and I thanked him. He then said, *"Ray, do you understand me?"* I said, *"Yes, he cannot have the second amended territory. We will go back to the former agreement."* He replied, *"I do not think you do understand. No means No. He will not have any amendment, there will be no franchise at all, in fact he will never be a part of our organisation."* My eyes were like one of those side show alley clowns all seeing and seeing nothing and my mouth would have perfectly fitted a ping pong ball. The Manager then looked hard at me and volunteered, *"Can you not see what I can with this person?"* What he was telling me was immediately apparent. If this person was someone who did not respect the agreement we had originally made and then agreed to amend, he would always be trying to exploit his position with our firm. When advised the client desperately pleaded to sign off on and even accept the original territory, but the door was now closed, forever. To me this was like being in the dark for so long and suddenly opening the curtains to broad, beautiful, daylight. I was inspired! Even though we would have liked the business and good operators like this man were hard to find, my company's values were inviolate and it is one of the main reasons it still flourishes and has been so respected for literally generations. To this day many young and old people cherish the possibility of eventually being employed by this firm with its strict honour in matters of values.

This was the finest company which I have ever worked. I recall quoting to every new Franchise office owner I appointed, again The Oracle of Omaha, Warren

Buffett, *"If you make a few mistakes, we will be very understanding, but if you bring our name into disrepute, we will be ruthless."* This always had a most sobering effect on the candidate in front of me. The management team and all the staff at this old firm were hand-picked people and so similar, like from the same family or template, straight, honourable folk, who one respected and admired. And at the top, was the example set by the bloke in the office with the old jarrah panelling and that *"hard eye"* who saw the truth every time. This company's staff lives their values of individual virtue and group goodwill. The firm is still part of the fabric of Australia. Companies like this make decisions and life much easier as there is never any compromising on integrity. The firm you offer your labour to will also contribute to the making of your character. Your values are never *"up for grabs"*.

Take a *"Message to Garcia"* and become passionately committed to your vocation. Getting the job done every day and being a respected, member of the team.

But the *"Sword of Damocles"* hangs over us all. I remember lying on my back on the beach making, *"sand angels"* thinking *"whattha duck!"* I had recently recorded a record profit in my division for the company, it was three weeks to Christmas and I was jobless! I had been *"freed up, let go, made redundant, restructured, downsized"* basically terminated which other state managers and myself had no influence on whatsoever. Well, I never saw that coming! Know your role will be compromised, for a multitude of reasons beyond your control and at some stage, probably more than once you will again be, *"out in the cold"*. But your resilience will carry you through, the experience will add value to you and you will accept, adapt, look back with no vindictiveness and even have a laugh as all part of the pathway. Oddly, often something even better says, *"Hi!"*

Remember you too, have choices of who you wish to serve as an employee, and it is important the people at the top are made of the sort of material that is consistent with your character, values and standards! You have every right to be discerning in places of employment as you have in your choice of friends and life partners.

The same rules apply to all of us in choosing your life companion, so how do you determine when you are madly in love if you are making the right choice? God only knows the answer to that one! So, give it up to him! Or if you really want to know, I can tell you a simple test to see if someone loves you. As in the words of another seven-year-old; *"You know when somebody loves you, their eyelashes go up and down and little stars come out of them."* So now you know!

I used to come into the office daily and half joke with my staff / colleagues Do **not forget** – *"everything speaks"*- Victor Hugo, which in terms we are discussing means:

- Were you on time today?
- Are you dressed like a professional?
- When you stand, stand straight never hands in pockets.
- Will you act with respect for all?
- Is your office / desk clear, neat and tidy?
- Will you be accountable for all your actions today?
- Will you get the job done today?

- Today will you willingly accept criticism?
- Can I stay non-judgemental?
- Are you relentlessly positive all day?

Everything you do is saying something, so just be aware – *"everything speaks."*

The former chief of the Australian Defence Force General David Hurley made a remarkable observation, which has now become a statement for our times, *"The standard you walk past is the standard you accept."* This is so powerful because it demands action from you. If you passively accept an action by someone that you know to be wrong in any aspect, then you are tacitly saying that conduct is acceptable to you. Indeed, you will be tested every day. For example, if you see some litter on the ground and you walk past you are accepting this as OK and your standard. The simplest way to say this is – RAISE YOUR STANDARDS. The US Navy Seal creed certainly encapsulates the right message. **"I serve with honour on and off the battlefield. The ability to control my emotions and my actions, regardless of circumstance, sets me apart from other men and women. Uncompromising integrity is my standard.**

My character and honour are steadfast. My word is my bond."

I was attending an evening club house function after a Rugby representative team selection trial in North Queensland and for some reason the captain of another club team, our arch enemies, decided to put one right on the nose of one of my players, who was a nice, quiet guy. I was shocked and being our team captain enquired from this man his justification for such an act, particularly off the field of play. He just smiled at me in defiance. He was a big bloke who had in a previous game broken the jaw of one of our front rowers who was too, an easy-going laconic man who always played the game straight and fair. So, we could say this other *"gentleman"* had a bit of a reputation. In fact, he was an outright bully. What should I do? There was considerable at stake here as he had obviously decided to belittle and intimidate our whole team.

As mentioned, I am convinced each of us have a few, that is three or four critical moments in our lives when we must make a hard call and our character is really tested. This may have been one of mine as I felt compelled to act in kind, knowing he would more than likely *"belt the daylights"* out of me. I extended an invitation to him to join me on the oval there and then. With about one hundred other players and supporters forming a circle around us, bare knuckle, no holds barred, we went at each other. He swore afterwards he would take his retribution and the following weekend we played their team with a notable, *"ring in."* I was on the bottom of a ruck receiving a good stomping from his team when I wore a full blown, deliberate boot in the side of the head from this new random player. The cut about two centimetres from the temple knocked me senseless and required twelve stitches. Lucky again, as a temple strike in martial arts is a last resort action. So, to some extent I suppose he did level the score. The point being in that previous situation, off the playing field, albeit back in wilder times I had to make a choice as the Captain of my team, to benignly accept that conduct or step up as a person with standards and speak the language he understood.

In hindsight I could have taken a deep breath and stoically told him in committing that act he has just incentivised our entire team and the next time we played, he and his team will know our will by us crushing them in every aspect of the game. Did I do the right thing in resorting to violence? I still ask myself this question. I do find some comfort in the words of one of the greatest advocates of nonviolence in history, Mahatma Gandhi in, "The Words of Gandhi" and I quote: *"I would rather India resort to arms in defence of her honour than she should in a cowardly manner become or remain a helpless witness to dishonour."* I do not for one moment suggest resorting to physical action unless you find yourself in that exceedingly rare circumstance when it is potentially a life-threatening situation for you or a friend and then you alone will have to make the call. Putting it in the simplest terms if you take one more thing from this handbook along with your never giving up and this is a tough one too. Let it be the words. ***"The standard you walk past is the standard you accept"*** and you will be OK.

Intriguingly we have different mindsets of high standards. I had a friend who was in Customer Service with the airline, doing shift work. When he came on duty the shared desk he used would be covered with dozens of cards and post-it stickers of unresolved matters his predecessor was actioning. John would carefully collate all this material, methodically gather it up into squared off, neat piles and then throw it all in the bin! For some not a recommended way of starting a shift but worked for him.

Have you ever noticed how some people are very meticulous? When they sit down, they arrange their pens carefully, their laptop in a particular position, raised to eye height, their notebook at the ready and even their back is straight! I will wager these people are more prepared than many others and that discipline gives them a slight edge. Remember, *"The way you do anything is the way you do everything,"* – Martha Beck.

I used to be what was called a *"spreader"* with non-important and non-urgent *"stuff"* spread literally around the perimeter of my desk. At least I looked busy! But oddly every single topflight operator and CEO I met had a spotless, clear desk all day every day. The number one daily step to efficiency? Make a list and prioritise. **Action the most important and urgent matter first** then file it to archive or secondly mark it for further investigation as a priority. What can be delegated, delegate and note to follow up. To be more accountable try to slow down a bit, focus and give yourself some tidiness and structure. Invoke the Pomodoro. Pay attention to your physical presentation, always start the day by making your bed, look at your goals, a clean desk and always standing straight (presence) and little by little you will see the benefits of slowly moving to a way where you are always more in control and thereby have less chances of negative outcomes.

I have the following statement framed on my desk at home, to constantly remind me of my accountability. It is a quotation from a Greek poet Archilochus more than 2500 years ago and reinforces doing the right thing every time is eternal. *"The fox knows many things, but the hedgehog knows one big thing."* It means the wily fox is so cunning, it knows many ways to catch the hedgehog, but the simple spiny hedgehog knows only one thing. If it rolls itself in a ball, no matter what the fox does it cannot touch the hedgehog.

Your values make you impenetrable. The simplicity of sticking with your standards turns you into a person of real strength. Someone to be respected

for your values and valued as a friend or a family member, an employee or employer. In other words, a person of good character particularly in tough times or a Paladin. I try to reach these standards and fall short over and over but I keep trying as that is all I can do. The following is an excerpt from a short story I read a long time ago which I often think about. You may find it illuminating too?

"The solar system, amidst a countless number of other systems as large as itself, rolls ever silently through space in the direction of the constellation of Hercules. The great spheres of which it is composed spin and spin through the eternal void ceaselessly and noiselessly. Of these one of the smallest and most insignificant is that conglomeration of solid and of liquid particles which we have named the Earth. It whirls onwards now as it has done before my birth and will do after my death — a revolving mystery, coming none know whence, and going none know whither. Upon the outer crust of this moving mass crawl many mites, of whom I, John Mc'Vittie, am one, helpless, impotent, being dragged aimlessly through space. Yet such is the state of things amongst us that the little energy and glimmering of reason which I possess is entirely taken up with the labours which are

necessary in order to procure certain metallic discs, wherewith I may purchase the chemical elements necessary to build up my ever-wasting tissues and keep a roof over me to shelter me from the inclemency of the weather. I thus have no thought to expend upon the vital questions which surround me on every side. Yet, miserable entity as I am, I can still at times feel some degree of happiness and am even – save the mark! – puffed up occasionally with a sense of my own importance." Sir Arthur Conan Doyle – *The Man from Archangel* 1885

The ability to endure seems vital to our intrinsic happiness Our story opened with an advertisement for crew from the great Sir Ernest Shackleton. You may now be able to relate a little better to this quote from his own book.

"South"

"We had pierced the veneer of outside things. We had suffered, starved and triumphed, grovelled down yet grasped at glory, grown bigger in the bigness of the whole. We had seen God in all his splendours. Heard the text that nature renders. We had reached the naked soul of man."

Summary:

- Understand some people will like you, some will not, and it is not your fault. You will be drawn to some people for what may be an inexplicable reason which is more than likely good for you, and they will feel the same.

- Your mind / conscience always knows the truth. Your ethics are not negotiable in any situation. Delay when confronted with a decision and watch the outcomes.

- Establish your values and know you will be tested over and over, and the muscle of integrity will grow.

- Be selective for whom you choose to work, the same with your friends.

- Being around good people with integrity will have its effect on you. You will be judged by the company you keep.

- I am aware of the dangers of gaming and social media influence on my wellbeing.

- Everything speaks. The way I look, act, do anything is the way I do everything. I prioritise tasks.

- The standard I walk past is the standard I accept.
- My values are immovable and make me stronger and a better person.
- I will slow down and be structured in all I say and do, I do not make excuses.
- I will stand up for what is right, sometimes alone, however when required I will act.
- My entire life is about everyday choices. Many will take courage. I always ask myself, "What is the right thing to do here?"

ACTION PLAN:

I am accountable and from now on I promise to make these actions part of my life as a person with values and review my performance monthly:

1..
....

2..
....

3..
....

4..
....

CHAPTER 13

WHAT DO I DO WHEN I FEEL ANXIOUS, LONELY OR DEPRESSED?

- A thought is only a thought it has no power. If it is a negative or *"what if"* thought observe it then say to yourself, *"OK you have made your self known now push it away and say GO"* My mind makes the decisions NOT my emotions. I observe my thoughts, consider and discard to make sure I never make an emotional based decision.

- I now know anxiety originates from the same region in my brain as excitement so I can easily say to myself. ***"I am excited by what is happening here, not anxious or fearful and look forward to the challenge!"***

- I will always have a good laugh at myself and the position I am in, knowing that will release some endorphins and relieve tension. As mentioned, **the** best natural tonic known to science to confront and reduce anxiety, pressure and anger is laughter. How? Just aloud do one Ha! Then two Ha, Ha. Then move onto three and right up to ten and you will be laughing. Laughter is one of the best medicines known.

- I can also go and **splash my face with cold water** to settle my heart rate – I may even say *"Very good"* a few times as there is a lesson being delivered to me.

- I knew this type of situation would come from time to time so **I am not surprised. I will do whatever I can. I may have to just ACCEPT and ADAPT and reset. I will remain stoic, indifferent, unmoved and not fix myself to the change or the feeling.** I can see the problem from outside looking in and know that in time I will recall and say, *"Wow, that was tough, but here I am."*

- I will use the deep breath method and just *"be"* for a moment, or even do a meditation or a prayer for a few minutes then assess the situation and do whatever I can to remedy it. **If there is no more I can** do, I will just give the outcome up to the universe and surrender to my higher power or God.

- I know there is a difference between being lonely and being alone **sometimes I enjoy being alone as a stoic and accepting the world and its challenging circumstances. And just being in the moment.**

- Mostly we feel lonely when people do not seem to understand how we feel. Then we wonder what is wrong with us. Well, nothing in fact as this is normal behaviour. We are all lonely from time to time. **Maybe our mind is suggesting we should stop and rest for a while. Plus, we have a goal to focus on.**

- **I will go for a run, or a walk, or a swim, or even a little skip along - as impossible to skip without smiling.** I know exercise is the best tonic when feelings start to overwhelm me. *"I must lose myself in action lest I wither in despair"*- Dale Carnegie. Go for a walk or do some exercise but get outside.

- Whatever happens. **I will not start** *"catastrophising"* **by overthinking things and allowing feelings of the past or impending doom to intrude in my thoughts.** I will cast out those thoughts and be present. I will sit and think of **three** things I can **see,** then three things I can **hear** and then three things I can **feel,** then do **two** things you can see, hear and feel, then **one** and the anxiety will minimise. Because you are placing yourself at rest, in the present.

- An amazing way to cheer myself up is to **reach out to another** soon as I can and offer my friendship and help.

- **I will speak to my Mentor or one of my best friends and share with them how I feel** as a problem shared is a problem half solved.

- *"This too shall pass"* **is an absolute truth.** All challenges in hindsight, strangely help me grow.

- **At any task I will commit totally to the action. I will not wander off thinking about other matters. I am** *"sweeping the temple"* **and in the moment.**

- **I never criticize or judge people. That sets me up for anxiety. I am mindful of my ego which is my pride, it wants control all the time leading to conflict. Pride cannot live with humility.**

CHAPTER 14

SAMPLE ACTION PLAN

1. **The past was just practice. I will never be a prisoner of my past.** Starting now I will act like a focussed but humble winner in every aspect of my life as I become what I think about. Today and every moment I am in the present that is what counts.

2. Make a short list of loyal friends and start building strong **lifelong friendships**.

3. *'The only thing that is keeping me from getting what I want, is the story I keep telling myself".* – Tony Robbins

4. Find a **mentor** who I can go to freely for advice.

5. Develop a can-do attitude by giving **everything I do everything I have** from this moment on. I also am **the best listener** I know. I never speak ill or put down others.

6. **Set my goals for the next six or twelve months**, lock them in, write the goals down, and how I am going to achieve them. Then measure myself.

7. Become a stoic in my mind and **indifferent by being resilient, always accepting outcomes and in control.** I am not impressed or concerned by circumstances beyond my control. I feel the pain of loss but **I know this too shall pass. What I can change I do what I cannot I accept and adapt.**

8. I am a Rock Breaker. I keep on swinging the hammer **I never quit as that is the only time I fail.** I am a trier who just never gives up. **I PRESS ON.**

9. **Find faith in a higher power** trusting that faith will deliver.

10. **Learn how to be still, breathe rest or quietly pray on a daily basis** and when I have no solution give it up to God or the universe.

11. **I am not a victim or a fool, I am a Leader.** My values and my friends identify me and my standards. I stand, even alone if I must, as that is how I am. I know the right thing to do when faced with a critical decision.

12. At the end of the day, I know 99% of people do not really give a *"flip"* about me. **I accept this. I know I will only ever really have my family and hopefully a few genuine, good friends. In particular with my future, sometimes good and bad decisions will be made and I will be part of those decisions. It will seem all my hard work will have been meaningless but that is never the case, my ability to endure will make the difference.**

13. I will make the principles of Micah 6: 8 a part of my life – **be fair, forgive show mercy and walk with humility.**

14. I am now a person of character and resilience and a leader **who thrives on discipline. My mind makes the decisions NOT my emotions.**

15. I know I will *"stuff up"* I will make mistakes but I will **learn the lesson** that is the crucial message. **I ACCEPT and ADAPT to situations.**

16. **I laugh in the face of adversity and keep laughing at life.**

17. *"People will forget what you said, people will forget what you did, but people will never forget how you made them feel."- Maya Angelou*

CHAPTER 15

HANDY TIPS FOR YOUR TOOLKIT

- After leaving school you will suddenly have a lot of time on your hands with no formalised structure and no one making demands on you to attend classes, even at University. When you do not have to attend tutorials there is no obligation to be anywhere at any time this is when many fail first year exams and are excused. You are now making most decisions on your own. That newfound freedom can be dangerous! **Do not under any circumstances sit around!** Doing nothing is a bad idea. Apart from the options mentioned previously like straight into work or travel, volunteering, job experience and TAFE. SET YOURSELF A GOAL. **Go and join a club**. Be it netball, football, surf lifesaving, whatever. **This is most important so you remain active.** Start mixing with older, more experienced successful people and creating good relationships for the future.

- Bullet-proofing – Your resume, cover letter and job application must be the best possible, otherwise the software packages mentioned earlier will reject you at first base. **You need to be totally cognizant with skillsroad.com.au; myfuture.edu.au; jobjumpstart.gov.au;** and how to step over the applicant tracking software systems **– jobscan.co**

- Your digital footprint must look like you are a superior applicant. A responsible, honourable person. As wherever you are on the Net you can be found. The employers have the ways and the means to find out who or what is behind that smiling sunny disposition!

- Find an idea of what type of career you like doing by trawling the web sites above then start applying. Simultaneously go and secure some volunteer work experience or ask your parents, use their referral contacts. Or work at Woolies or Coles. This is crucial as **the only time to get a job is when you have a job, even volunteering.** Now be the absolute best you can here because this is your first reference. Plus, often you end up being offered a permanent role in any case.

- You do not get a second chance at a good first impression. Studies have realised 55% of a favourable impression is made in first few seconds, another 38% in first sentences spoken. That is 93% of starting off well or smashing into the first hurdle.

- The job interview: **Everything speaks** – head up, look and dress the part. Take three deep breaths before you go in and say to yourself, *"I am excited."* Be confident and enthusiastic. One of the first questions I would always ask an applicant is, *"Tell me what you know about our company?"* If the applicant stumbled on this question, the interview did not take long. The company website is a good place to start with this one. Remember the six P's. Do the research. What are the corporate aims and values, why would you want to work here? Address every requirement / qualification in the JD, (job description). **What can you bring to the table?** This book should give you some answers to that one. Give examples of objectives set and achieved or reasons not completed but your capacity to press on. You are always on time. You can Take a Message to Garcia. Give me the job or task and it will be completed no questions asked. Be prepared for the, *"Tell me about you,"* question. *"What are your three best strengths?"* You already have these attributes. Examples of turning a calamity into an opportunity. You need to apply for the role for the right reasons too and have the reasons. Plus, answer, *"What you will bring to the company."*

The interview goes two ways. So, wait until the interviewer asks; *"Any questions about the position?"* Then ask **a few** of the following which you have typed on a sheet of paper:

➤ May I ask how did this role become available?

➤ If I were successful what would be the most important thing to achieve in the first six months? Apart from still being here! (joke)

➤ What would outstanding performance look like in this role?

➤ Can you tell me what the career paths are for this role and what sort of advancements I could work towards?

➤ Is there any company capability for further training for example if one had University aspirations?

- ➢ Can you tell me what are the most common characteristics you are seeking in this role and do you feel I may have those qualities?
- ➢ What do you love the most about working here?
- ➢ May I ask what are the next steps in the interview process?
- ➢ Is there anything else I can provide you with that would be helpful or questions that I can answer whilst I am here?

- **Role play your interview** with someone else until you become competent. A little tip: when you leave the office make sure you email the interviewer and thank them for the opportunity of being considered and ensure the management of your enthusiasm for the role. This not only shows that you are polite, but it also puts your name in front of the interviewer again, especially if they have interviewed others after you.
- The best sounding word to anybody in the world is their own name. Whenever you meet anyone and engaging in a conversation **make a point of addressing them by their name every time you**

speak to the other person. Practice this and watch the response, it is always appreciated and shows your respect.

- If you want an edge to win someone to your way of thinking in a negotiation, say *"Your point is well made but I need some help here please can you explain further OR at a certain level I totally agree but can you help clarify…...?"*

- If physically confronted by a bully step back, face them, look them right in the eye and smile. Say, *"OK I heard you, yes some of what you say is true" or say, "Very good thanks for the criticism."* Then find something nice to say to them like, *"You know what …… I have always admired you for this reason- popularity, sports ability, confidence, cool gear you wear etc."* This is called emotional intelligence. **No one who is really confident and happy is unkind to others.** If someone is mean that is because someone or something has previously frightened them. You could look at them and say with empathy, *"Who hurt you?"* You see hurt people hurt people. Or *"R U OK?"* You can make the same responses over the "Net". If you are respectfully honest that will disarm them every time. By engaging the other party and being genuine, they will more than likely reach out to you as these people certainly need friends. In a physical environment ideally a friend will come up say nothing and stand beside you.

- If the aggressor keeps coming, face them and shout out as loud as you can **"STOP!"** If they persist place both hands open and arms stretched out front and say, *"If you touch me forcibly in any way, without my consent that is assault."* If not then RUN!

- **Only in extreme situations break the chain of command and bypass your superior.** Always go through your direct supervisor – it is usually self-limiting to overstep your Form Teacher/Manager. Respect demands that you speak or share your idea or concerns with this person first. Recognition will happen just keep thinking and looking with fresh eyes and the ideas and success will blossom.

- **If you raise a problem, it is better to always have the solution too,** never just throw up a negative or complaining statement. Present the problem and provide your suggested solution or it is best to be silent until you have thought of a viable solution.

- When asked, *"How are you?"* Which you will be every day of your life, never ever say *again,* *"OK, good, not bad (note the double negative) or all right."* Pick one of the statements below and make that your own or make your own up. Your response from today onwards could be something like:- ***"Terrific and you – never better and you – sensational you – raring to go and how are you – relentlessly positive – going to Defcon 2 – bulletproof - today I am a coconut but tomorrow an orange – outstanding – a few cuts and bruises but nothing I cannot handle – I am fired with enthusiasm,"*** because if you are not as previously mentioned, fired with enthusiasm, you know what happens…

- To be successful in school or business here is a guaranteed winning tip from a multi–millionaire I know: **"Just be in the office or if work from home be operational at 8am every day and always be the last to leave or log out.** You see in this time you will prepare your day ahead and you will be amazed how much you can achieve in a quiet relaxed environment. Or spend an hour in the library after school giving you an edge every time preparing for tomorrow. Plus, the right people will notice and respect your diligence and will be there to support you when you need it. If working, you also dodge the traffic. I met many fascinating people in the office after hours like GM's curiously strolling the corridors and equally interesting, nearly every night cleaner, for every company I ever worked.

- Whenever anyone **asks for a volunteer, quietly put your hand up.** Not in a grandstanding way but showing a little humility as if to say, *"I will give it a go."* Volunteer for every task as **leaders always go first** and we love discipline and the commitment as we know it is good for us.

- My grandson was eight years old and I asked him, *"Mate, don't you ever get tired?"* He said, *"No I run at 100% all the time, if I do go down to ninety-five percent, I have a little rest for five minutes and then I am back to 100%."* From the mouth of babes! Performing **the Pomodoro Technique** and does not even know it.

- **Never be late or too early for an appointment**. You are always on time. Many think 5 or 10 minutes late is acceptable – it is not. You are always on time or late.

- **The person who actively listens is the person who earns respect. I never judge others, I am non-judgemental, I remain silent!**

- *"It is the backup that will beat them every time."* That is a Rugby phrase which holds perfectly in life, **always follow up,** be relentless and never assume the job has been completed. Ask, *"Just seeking an update"* tactfully and quietly until the matter is concluded.

  - **Never stop reading.** It will fast track you in so many ways. The key to success is knowledge and knowledge is found in reading from those who have experienced more than we ever will and had the generosity to share.

  - It is far easier to stay out of trouble than to get out of trouble.

  - **PTG – *"Play the game,"* accept the bad outcomes.** Understand that schools and big corporations have their idiosyncrasies accept that and be compliant but never compromise your ethics. **Do not be the joker or the wild one or the stirrer.** Play a team game and be a strong part of the team despite times when you feel something does not suit you. Just take it on the chin and be stoic and laugh. Management seeks out the tough individuals who are stoic and can, *"cop it sweet."* You adapt to situations.

- When the dark shadow of depression comes calling, sit and ask now what can I learn from this visit? Why am I feeling this way?

- A true friend walks in when the entire world walks out. *"Life is mostly froth and bubble. Two things stand like stone – kindness in another's trouble and courage in your own"*- Adam Lindsay Gordon. **Be a bankable commodity as a loyal friend.**

- **Never ever send an emotional email or text or make a phone call or talk when you are not in complete control of your emotions.** Breathe, you are far better letting the other party talk/tweet themselves to a standstill every time.

- When about to be asked something by your superior, sometimes even before the actual question is put to you, in a jovial way respond, *"The answer is yes, now what is the question?"* You are saying, I can do it, I am taking on the challenge whatever it may be.

- I met a wonderful elderly gentleman, Bob Hamilton when I embarked on my carbon paper career, Bob told me one day whilst banging his knuckles on my little desk to ram home his point, some words I have never forgotten. *"I know men in the ranks who will stay in the ranks. Why? Because they do not have the ability to get things done."* Dale Carnegie – *Just do the job required in the time allocated* with no questions, as the vast majority cannot accept the given task and – *just do it.* He was the person who gave me A Message To Garcia

- Never have anybody ask you, *"Can you do better than this?"* Be like the good carpenter, measure twice cut once, so every job is your best.

- If you want somebody to do something for you explain the reason do not just instruct them. I learned in management a quick explanation as to WHY makes all the difference in getting things done.

- Never join the gossipers or the merchants of misery. A sure-fire way to demolish your credibility is the moment you say you agree with vexatious gossip about someone else. You are non-judgemental. **If you cannot say something positive about someone – say nothing.**

- **We can rationalize anything to our benefit.** Generally, it is trying to substantiate a case to do something dumb that we know already is a *"baaaad idea."* So many times, over the years I have heard; *"Just try it once. Or what they do not know cannot hurt them. You can afford it. I will not tell a soul. Just for an hour. No one will get hurt."* And so on like those silly rites of passage. Do not become trapped into this game. You are in charge of you.

- **Tattoos are a personal choice – for life.** I would suggest before committing buy a little time, sleep on it and then decide the next morning – after breakfast. If you are still convinced so be it. As you now **I never act on emotional impulses,** use your mind to make decisions. A thought – Why do you think you never see a bumper sticker on a Ferrari?

- When there seemed to be an error of significance made by someone else, I learned to always say to the staff member, *"I know there is a very good reason why you did that, I just cannot wait to hear it."* **There are two sides to every story so avoid drawing any conclusion until you have heard from all parties.** As often, the other party will have a particularly good explanation for their actions.

- Stay aware but not aloof. You are always in control. **You are your own person, a stoic and indifferent to outside circumstances.**

- Quitting gets easier all the time and is so contagious!

- It takes courage to trust people. A few of those you trust will let you down, your friends may do so too and you will be taken advantage of as that is the way of the world. And it sure hurts. You too will let others down. **Apart from family and one or two friends no one gives a flip about me.**

- How do you tell when someone is making something up? Or telling a fib when answering a question from you? The jury is divided. Criminal analysts assert they may ask you to repeat the question or put a hand to their face. NLP has worked for me in discussions for years or even watching interviews on TV. Up to you to give it a try. (*Frogs to Princes* by Bandler and Grinder).

- **Join a club** that has a common interest to yours it matters not how capable you are just do it, get involved in an activity outside work or school. This is most important.

- *"Press On"* and *"this too shall pass"* have solved and always will solve every problem you face.

- Your problem will never be the doing **it will always be the thinking of the doing.** Reading and running must be part of your life.

- Your mind must be stronger than your feelings. **Every poor decision will always come from emotion** rather than from your mind.

- Your toughest achievements will be the most worthwhile, your most loyal people will be the hardest to win over, **your greatest challenge will be you.**

- The US Navy Seals have a saying *"slow is smooth, smooth is fast."* Watch Kathy Freeman winning the 2000 Olympic 400 metres. Mentally in total control but running effortlessly. The best of all of us develop this skill and apply it daily in all types of actions. Still working on it!

- **Attend a jobs expo** to get a feel for different vocations.

- After Year 12 have a look at enrolling in the Year13.com.au or rfttejobs.com programme or just travel. **You have earned it!**

- **I always pay myself first. 10% of my take home pay goes in a separate Bank account I never touch.**

- Gambling is for losers only, do not touch it.

- You will be offered a credit card. If you accept put a limit of $1000 on it and **do not increase it.**

- **Pay the credit card off in full every month without fail** – this is establishing your credit rating you are being monitored!

- Never borrow to buy furniture or appliances or stuff because you will be paying hard finance rates of 16-18% despite all the interest free offers the outstanding amount compounds on a severely depreciating asset.

- **A good question to ask yourself before that impulsive buy is, "Do I need this or do I only want this or do I need and want this?"**

- Stay at home as long as you can and sock it away like a squirrel!

- **To buy a car get a personal loan from a Bank – and pay it off before the end of the term!!! Now you have a good credit rating.**

- Set annual goal to reward yourself with fun or trip NOT to a Casino!

- Budget a monthly spend on stuff and make it last, once spent it is over.

- Oscar Wilde said, *"Some cause happiness wherever they go; others whenever they go."* The choice is yours.

- You have two minds the OBSERVER and the monkey mind always worrying you with *"what if"* thoughts. Recognise and then push those worrying controlling ego driven thoughts away and stay in the present reality. With every action totally focus on the task alone. Not easy but you are running the show and the benefits are wonderful.

- Learn to sit and be and focus on your breath in and out and nothing else and ask God to come into your life.

- Why do we all seem to want more and more of what we don't need?

- A father said to his young teen three statements to finish every morning:

"Knowledge is what?" the response, **"Power"**.

"The more you learn, the more you?" **"Earn"**.

"I never". **"Give Up"**.

This mantra will set you on the right path.

- You may feel I have been a little too repetitive on a few skills. That is deliberate as I too embrace the Rule of Seven. **These skills are proven and like granite blocks can become the foundations of your future happiness.** Set them deep and well and you will become the best person you can be.

- Look up **myfuture.edu.au/bullseyes** to give you an idea of careers

CHAPTER 16

My Words of Honour

Please do not underestimate the power of this request. I would like you to create up to eight words as your personal promise of how you intend to face your life. A bit like a Mantra (the word Mantra comes from the Indian Sanskrit meaning a "sacred message or counsel"). Once decided, write it down and carry it with you. My own was, "I am calm, relaxed and in complete control." Always worked when I remembered to use it! Feel happy to share with your mentor, your best friend, your parents or even daily with your hardest task master your own self and then review your performance weekly.

Examples which may give you some ideas:

- I never, never, never, never, never, give up
- This too shall pass
- Those who endure call the whole world brother
- I try to make everyone I meet feel valued
- I the power that feeling uncomfortable gives me
- It's never what happens it's how I choose to react
- My mind not my feelings always makes the calls
- How I do anything is how I do everything

- I stop think and never complain or judge
- I am indifferent to circumstances.
- What I cannot change I accept and adapt
- My goals give my life meaning and purpose
- I WILL SURRENDER TO MY HIGHER POWER

CHAPTER 17

THE THREE FROGS

Well, there you have it my friends, young Paladins. Throughout my life I have been learning and trying to actively apply the above principles. I can also attest every time I have made a severe error, there is a line leading straight to a direct breach of the skills shared with you in this book. I hope I have answered a few questions that you may have and even raised a few new questions for you to ponder?

I honestly wish I had this skill set in my pocket to review in Year 12 when feeling so alone on the last day of school and I started the long walk to the bus stop and into the big, wide, wonderful world. I have made a multitude of mistakes, many more than once, but I persist to this day and luck has followed me with a great life, a wonderful loving family and five of the best friends one could ask for.

If, starting now you embrace these skills, you may ask what is the payoff for you? I am convinced financially you will be more secure and be able to enjoy more of life's tangible offerings. You will receive the goodwill of others, thereby making your life more satisfying. But even more important than either of the afore mentioned you will be in touch with the infinite. How? You will know.

I had walked up the hill to the church near our school bus stop many, many times as a boy. This time I parked my car. My Dad, who was also my best mate, did not come through his fourth *"last rites"* benediction in November 1982. St. Stephens Church remained unchanged but inside, in this case was vastly different. Never had I seen so many people attend the church. Dad's friends were literally in every pew, all along the side walls and filling the entrance foyer even overflowing out the doors. I knew a few of the grim, stoic, faces from other times. Times when I knew his friends, when there was always laughter. Many others, I never had the privilege to meet and were complete strangers. After the funeral one of his best mates, Bill Clarke pulled me aside and said, *"Son, if you can be half of the man your father was, you will be OK."* Interestingly after Dad's funeral Bill and Irene Clarke called over to

Mum's house in Coorparoo every single Tuesday night for seven years until Mum moved to the Gold Coast. Now that is a devoted friend. As Dad had told me at twenty, I was a *"mug."* My Mum told me Dad was proud of me, but I wish it were him who had told me, just once.

On that overcast, bleak day which became such surf club folklore, we even gave it a name; *"The day of the Bombora."* The wave had come a long way from the blue deep to finally tear itself apart in that place, at that moment. I had drifted away from the pack as I was never quite, *"one with the water,"* like some the others who were also Australian champions. But this one it was all set up for me. Alone in two strokes as it stood up, I was on the cap of the monstrous swell, peaking, still for a moment in time, when I knew I was committed. Then I was falling through space as the pent-up energy of cyclonic winds exploded with tons of water. There were three in the set, if there had been a fourth, who knows, as after the second crashed on me I could no longer dive deep and was literally fighting for my life. A bit like opening the sluice gates on a dam and from clear water suddenly sucked downwards into a churning maelstrom full of sand, no sound or light and no way to know which way was up. Held deep down swimming desperately any which way lungs screaming for air. I remember being cast onto the beach face down, hands squeezing the sand thinking a moment before, how close I was to breathing water and drowning. A defining moment? Was that leviathan from the deep made to push me for the first time into the abyss, to be broken and yet somehow to make me a little bit stronger than before, to prepare me like Kintsugi?

Thank you so much for coming on this personal journey with me. I would like to think you are becoming a stoic person, non-judgemental and humble. The first to always forgive and even, if the last to always finish.

In retrospect as I learned these skills, they seemed to pay unforeseen dividends, good things and success started coming my way, friends would say to me you are so lucky, strange as if the universe does love a trier. I would wager the same will happen with you. There were three frogs on a log. One decided to jump off. How many were left? Two? No there were still three, that one had only decided to jump. **Now will you set goals, commit to them and jump or just decide?** By the way I enjoy frequently opening a page of this booklet to remind myself too - to practice what I preach. May I ask what are you waiting for? You are about to author your own story. Are you prepared to pay the ransom of these skills to change the rest of your life? Your future is yours to claim, so go and seize it!

Let us cast aside our excuses and embrace the power of our own, *"words of honour"*. Let us forge a path of strength and resilience, a path of courage and determination. For we are the masters of our fate the captains of our souls and nothing can hold us back from our objectives. Good luck and I sincerely hope you find a life full of happiness and even discover the elusive key - Grace.

May your frog grow feathers and you find *"five of the best"* too. Friends that is! Because everything that has happened to you up to now was just practice. You now have what **IT** takes. You have made the best investment you ever will, in your own good self. Perhaps one day someone may look you in the eye and say, *"Because of you, I never gave up."*

Invictus by William Henley

Out of the night that covers me,
Black as the Pit from pole to pole,
I thank whatever gods may be
For my unconquerable soul.

In the fell clutch of circumstance
I have not winced nor cried aloud.
Under the bludgeoning's of chance
My head is bloody, but unbowed.

Beyond this place of wrath and tears
Looms but the Horror of the shade,
And yet the menace of the years
Finds, and shall find, me unafraid.

It matters not how strait the gate,
How charged with punishments the scroll,
I am the master of my fate:
I am the captain of my soul.

RECOMMENDED READING:

Below is a selection of books in no particular order, for you to consider. Most are not too long and pack a fine message, a few you can download as a PDF. I am confident you will enjoy these stories, make you think and perhaps help you understand a little more about your good self. Of course, my aim is to turn you onto reading for life because readers become leaders.

- A Message to Garcia by Elbert Hubbard (short story PDF online)
- The Three Hermits by Leo Tolstoy (short story PDF online)
- Courage under Fire by James Stockdale
- The Outsider / The Stranger by Albert Camus
- The Old Man and the Sea by Ernest Hemingway
- How to Build a Fire by Jack London (short story PDF online)
- The Life of Pi by Yann Martel
- Call of the Wild by Jack London
- Being There by Jerzy Kosinski
- When the Lion Feeds by Wilbur Smith
- Man's Search for Meaning by Viktor Frankl
- Kane and Abel by Jeffrey Archer
- The Prophet by Kahlil Gibran
- How to Stop Worrying and Start Living by Dale Carnegie
- Angela's Ashes by Frank McCourt
- How to Win Friends and Influence People by Dale Carnegie
- The Hobbit by JJR Tolkien

- For the Term of his Natural Life by Marcus Clark
- Ajahn Brahm (You Tube)
- The Dead by James Joyce (short story PDF online)
- Endurance by Alfred Lansing
- How Much Land Does a Man Need? by Leo Tolstoy (short PDF online)
- A Fortunate Life by Albert Facey
- Flowers for Algernon by Daniel Keys
- The Goshawk by TH White
- The Master and Margarita by Mikhail Bulgakov
- Moby Dick by Herman Melville
- The Road Less Travelled by M. Scott Peck
- Any problems with acquiring copies try Amazon online
- and of course, a walk and a jog / sprint between streetlights for 30 minutes twice a week!

Acknowledgements:

Adrian Pree Headmaster St. James Anglican School for his initial support and encouragement

Bronwyn Smith Humanities Teacher Alkimos Baptist College for her excellent advice on visual presentations and constructive feedback

Bruce Pascoe Author "Finding Courage" for final editing and proof reading

UWA - Peter Sinden Senior Lecturer Law Faculty

Wendy and Prof. Stephen Powles UWA for their encouragement and editing in improving the manuscript

Rachael Kohn for her incisive constructive advices with early draft

Frank Douglas, Owen Puie (Club Captain), Andre Van Muren (the Dutchman), Jim Abbott (Boat Captain) Peter Williams (Sweep) and Ray (The Penguin) Mac Donald surf swimmer, beltman - NBSLSC for allowing me to quote the personal anecdotes

Mike (cop it sweet) Thies our Premiership Captain GPS Rugby Union and Peter Bisset who wrote our club song – The Finsbury Girls

Jenny and Greg Lawson reviewing the draft and their ongoing support

Major Ross Crunkhorn AIF sharing The Ten Principles of Warfare

Rechelle Hawkes Olympic champion for her kind permission to refer to her outstanding achievements

Jonas Pampel Holocaust survivor and my old workout companion RIP

Peter Maxwell State Manager Elders Limited for his inspiring leadership

Steve Missen (don't call my card) Boxer

Sgt. Alan Bennett Welsh Guards Falklands War

Brian Anderson NZ World Cup Rugby League Team, First grade North Sydney Rugby League, NSW Country – Mana

Especially my wife Arlene whose diligence and critique required considerable effort and in doing so was an act of love and true resilience.

Notes:

www.ingramcontent.com/pod-product-compliance
Lightning Source LLC
Chambersburg PA
CBHW071313090426
42738CB00012B/2692